States and Tribes

Building New Traditions

A broad examination of the condition of state-tribal relations and opportunities for mutually beneficial cooperation as the 21st century approaches, from a state legislative policy perspective

Prepared at the direction of the
NCSL Task Force on State-Tribal Relations
Senator Bob Jauch and Senator Enoch Kelly Haney, Co-Chairmen

Compiled and edited by
James B. Reed, Program Principal
Judy A. Zelio, Senior Policy Specialist

National Conference of State Legislatures
William T. Pound, Executive Director
1560 Broadway, Suite 700
Denver, Colorado 80202

444 North Capitol Street, N.W., Suite 515
Washington, D.C. 20001

November 1995

The National Conference of State Legislatures serves the legislators and staffs of the nation's 50 states, its commonwealths, and territories.

NCSL was created in January 1975 from the merger of three organizations that served or represented state legislatures. NCSL is a bipartisan organization with three objectives:

- To improve the quality and effectiveness of state legislatures,
- To foster interstate communication and cooperation,
- To ensure states a strong cohesive voice in the federal system.

The Conference operates from offices in Denver, Colorado, and Washington, D.C.

Cover Art: *Freedom's Vision* by renowned Seminole-Creek artist and Oklahoma state Senator Enoch Kelly Haney. Courtesy of the Haney Art Gallery, Shawnee, Oklahoma, (405) 275-2270.

Printed on recycled paper

CONTENTS

PREFACE

In early 1990, concerned state legislators came together as members of the National Conference of State Legislatures (NCSL) Task Force on State-Tribal Relations. They sought new approaches to state-tribal relations and wanted to publicize effective working relationships and agreements between Indian tribes and state governments. The time was ripe for such an examination. Forces of cooperation and of division were receiving great public scrutiny. Task forces and working groups of other organizations emerged at about the same time to address concerns related to treaty rights, sovereignty, and government-to-government relations. The NCSL task force and its staff received funding from the Ford Foundation to conduct a survey and publish a report on state-tribal relations, as well as arrange 12 meetings around the country and publish briefing papers. Many people including state legislators, legislative staff, Indian commission members, tribal members, staff of tribal associations, regional and state association staff, federal officials, and others were consulted for the report. The acknowledgments contain a partial list of those who assisted this important effort.

In Boise and Orlando, San Diego and Washington, D.C., Phoenix and Portland, Maine, the task force heard from people who spoke eloquently of tribal sovereignty, gaming, nuclear waste disposal, government-to-government relations, state-tribal agreements, taxes, the arts, education, and the "next 500 years." We have attempted to collect the wisdom and perspective of those speakers to shed light on the condition of state-tribal relations and combine it with research findings from traditional sources and survey findings.

Cooperative state-tribal government relationships are difficult to establish. With slim guidance from the U.S. Constitution and inconsistent foundations in case law, states and tribes are forging their ways in a legal wilderness. The primary government-to-government relationship for most tribes is at the federal level. Because of ill-defined relationships and imprecise definitions of regulatory authority, state and Indian tribal governments are often on their own to work out one-to-one arrangements.

Nonetheless, many achievements are apparent. Hundreds of intergovernmental agreements have forged workable relationships. Each new agreement strengthens the foundation of state-tribal law. State legislatures are important forums for determining such agreements as evidenced by the doubling of state-tribal legislation considered over the past five years. Cooperative relationships are critical as states and Indian nations face deep federal budget cuts, block grants, and other national policy changes in 1995 and beyond.

Successful working relationships between state and tribal governments are the focus of our report. The first three chapters present an overview of state-tribal issues focusing on the dilemma of "nations amidst the states." The next seven chapters present discussions of particular issues including education, health care, child welfare, economic development, gaming, taxation, natural resource management, and environmental regulation. The report closes with recommendations for improving state-tribal relations.

The book does not address law enforcement, cultural and religious freedom, reburial and repatriation issues, and energy development. Law enforcement is discussed by the Commission on State-Tribal Relations in *State-Tribal Agreements* which summarizes 30 state-tribal agreements. The Native American Rights Fund has done significant work on issues of religious freedom and repatriation, and the spring 1993 issue of *Natural Resources and Environment*, published by the American Bar Association, looks thoroughly at energy development.

We have consulted with members of our task force and tribal members regarding the use of the terms "Indians," "Native Americans," "American Indians," "Natives," and "Native American Indians" and were informed that each is acceptable. The terms are used interchangeably throughout the report. The designations refer to those people who are acknowledged members of tribes, as determined by individual tribal governments.

The NCSL State-Tribal Relations Task Force has had an impact. State policies in California, Maine, Montana, New Mexico, New York, Oklahoma, South Dakota, Wisconsin, and Wyoming have been affected by lawmakers or staff who have participated in task force activities. Within NCSL, the task force recommended that tribal issues be formally included within the jurisdiction of a standing committee, and this was accomplished. Much remains to be done, but NCSL, with generous support from the Ford Foundation, has helped foster an enlightened attitude that nurtures negotiated approaches to state-tribal disputes that serve, ultimately, to strengthen the nation's democratic fabric.

References

American Bar Association. *Natural Resources and Environment* 7, no. 4 (Spring 1993).

Commission on State Tribal Relations. *State-Tribal Agreements: A Comprehensive Study.* Albuquerque: American Indian Law Center; and Denver: National Conference of State Legislatures, 1983.

Native American Rights Fund. "Congress Overturns Supreme Court's Peyote Ruling." *Legal Review* 20, no. 1 (Winter/Spring 1995).

Pommersheim, Frank, "Tribal State Relations: Hope for the Future?" *South Dakota Law Review* 36, no. 2 (1990).

ACKNOWLEDGMENTS

This book represents the collaboration and inspiration of literally hundreds of people, most of whom had the time and opportunity to say what they needed to say. We were not forced to meet artificial deadlines, thanks to the understanding of our Ford Foundation program officers, Lynn Walker and Anthony Romero and grants administrators Doris Keniry and Mary Lopez. The NCSL Task Force on State-Tribal Relations served as the guiding force behind this effort under the visionary leadership of Senator Bob Jauch of Wisconsin and Senator Enoch Kelly Haney of Oklahoma. In the task force's early days, Senator Delwyn Gage of Montana, Senator James Dunn of South Dakota, and Representative Albert Shirley of New Mexico provided similar guidance. Task force members who contributed very significantly included the late Priscilla Attean, Penobscot Tribal Representative of Maine; Representative Larry Gabriel of South Dakota; the late Emil Grieser, Oklahoma state representative; Representative Ben Hanley of Arizona; Senator Georgianna Lincoln of Alaska; former state senator, now Congressman Jack Metcalf of Washington; Representative Lynda Morgan of New Mexico; Representative Scott Ratliff of Wyoming; and Senator Paul Valandra of South Dakota. The appendix provides a complete list of task force members.

Dozens of participants in the 12 meetings of the task force shaped, nurtured, and focused the outcome this book represents. A number deserve particular mention for providing extra support and advice: Michelle Aguilar, Representative Tom Atcitty, Representative Shirley Baca, Michael Cox, Debbie Dahlhaus, Roxanne Davis, Joseph DeLaCruz, Representative Bill Dover, Richard DuBey, Harley Duncan, Doug Endreson, Connie Erickson, Bill Gollnick, Kevin Gover, Tassie Hanna, LaDonna Harris, Robert Holden, Judith Holm, Representative Jack Jackson, Senator Dan Jerome, Yvette Joseph, Yvonne Kauger, Rick Keister, Tony Machukay, Wilma Mankiller, Representative Roger Madalena, Senator Joe Mazurek, Eddye McClure, Dwight McKay, Clinton Pattea, Browning Pipestem, Marshall Plummer, Pam Ray, Representative Angela Russell, Nick Salazar, Pam Shannon, Passamaquoddy Tribal Representative Madonna Soctomah, Shirley Solomon, Mervyn Tano, Harold Tarbell, Derrick Watchman, the late Representative Leo Watchman, and Patricia Zell. Ernest LaBelle of TRW, Inc. attended nearly every meeting as the State Government Affairs Council liaison to the task force, and along with Tina Wall and Derek Crawford of Philip Morris, provided support for several working lunches.

David Getches, David Lester, and David Lovell deserve special thanks for their very thoughtful written comments and suggestions about this book. Others who kindly have provided guidance when asked for advice include Jo Clark, John Echohawk, Larry EchoHawk, Lucille Echohawk, Walter Echo Hawk, gaiashkibos, Nelson Kempsky, Sarge Waukau, and Tim Wapato.

We truly appreciate the 80 participants in our state-tribal survey. Their honest answers provided the basis for chapter 2 and helped complement our book research with on-the-ground experience.

A team of NCSL staff researched and wrote this book. Contributors include Kate Mahoney, chapter 2; Lucinda Bryant and Terry Whitney, chapter 4; Jackie Cummins, chapter 5; Rebecca Weiss, chapters 8 and 9; Mara Cohen, chapter 9; James B. Reed, preface, chapters 1, 2, 3, 5, 8, 9 and 10; and Judy Zelio, chapters 1, 3, 4, 6, 7, 8, and 10. David Lester, Council of Energy Resource Tribes, contributed an essay for chapter 5. Dwight Connor,

Corina Eckl, Jon Felde, Pam Greenberg, Tracey Hooker, Susan Johnson, Jeanne Mejeur, Larry Morandi, Dan Pilcher and Ronald Snell of NCSL provided helpful comments throughout. NCSL staff who assisted at various stages of producing the book include Carolyn Alvarez, Sia Davis, Michelle Pavlock, and Leann Stelzer. Karen Hansen and Karen Fisher were supportive editors. As lead authors, Jim Reed and Judy Zelio wish to thank Diane Chaffin, Karl Kurtz, and Bill Pound for their unwavering support of this effort. The authors apologize for the inevitable errors and omissions.

Highlights

Chapter 1: The Nations Amidst the States

- States and tribes exist as mutual sovereigns, sharing contiguous geographic areas and common citizens.

- Indian tribal populations and economic power are growing and increasing the importance of state-tribal relations.

- Tribal lands occupy a unique niche in the legal arena.

- Tribal responsibilities take into account treaties with the U.S. government.

- Treaty rights and federal trust responsibilities affect state-tribal interactions.

- States and tribes sometimes take different approaches to meeting the needs of their citizens. Cooperation between states and tribes is impeded by murky legal relationships and conflict over treaties.

Chapter 2: Survey of State-Tribal Relations

- Tribal sovereignty is at the core of many state-tribal misunderstandings.

- Communication between states and tribes needs improvement.

- State and tribal officials support written cooperative agreements.

- Working together on less controversial issues builds the capacity to work cooperatively on tougher subjects in the future.

- Survey respondents listed dozens of successful state-tribal agreements.

Chapter 3: Seeking Common Ground Through State-Tribal Agreements

- State legislatures offer a meeting place for states and tribes to interact.

- Sovereign governments must continually sort out responsibilities.

- When states and tribes disagree, options for resolution include negotiated settlements, mediated agreements, and litigation.

- Intergovernmental agreements are positive, practical approaches for states and tribes to use in resolving jurisdictional disagreements.

- Endeavors to improve governmental relationships may help "reinvent government."

Chapter 4: State Roles in Indian Health, Education, and Child Welfare

- The national Indian Health Service, which is part of the U.S. Public Health Service, is responsible for many tribal members' health care.

- States also play a significant role in health care services to Indian people under Medicaid and through private providers, but statistics do not identify Indian recipients separately from other citizens.

- The rates of alcoholism-related illnesses and accidents, tuberculosis, and diabetes are high for Indian populations.

- State initiatives in the area of Indian health care appear to be limited, but several states have worked to improve Indian education.

- States play the major role in the formal education of Native American children.

- A national report called "Indian Nations at Risk" has identified ways that states can improve their educational efforts for Native Americans.

- Several states have made strides in improving Native American education.

- Tribal colleges offer an alternative to Indian people who desire higher education.

- Under the federal Indian Child Welfare Act, states and tribes must try to keep Indian children under the care of Indian people, particularly members of their tribes.

Chapter 5: State-Tribal Economic Development Partnerships

- Tribes are striving to increase their economic self-sufficiency.

- Both state and the national governments have roles in supporting tribal economic development.

- Many tribes depend on tourism as economic development.

- Natural resources form the basis for much tribal economic development.

- Strong tribal economies add strength to state economies.

Chapter 6: States and the Indian Gaming Regulatory Act

- Gaming has proved to be successful economic development for some tribes.

- Some states and tribes differ over the types of gaming that should take place within a state's borders.

- The federal Indian Gaming Regulatory Act prescribes a process by which states and tribes can resolve their differences.

- Over 150 state-tribal gaming compacts have been completed.

- State legislatures are increasing their involvement in developing gaming compacts.

- Experience in communication between state legislators and tribal leaders on a variety of issues facilitates discussions on other controversial issues like gaming.

Chapter 7: Seeking Agreement on Taxes

- Generally, tribes, like other government entities, are exempt from federal taxation.

- Generally, states may not impose taxes on tribal lands or on tribal members whose income derives from tribal employment.

- Generally, tribal members do pay taxes on purchases, income, and other activity that takes place off Indian lands.

- State-tribal tax agreements increasingly are used to resolve questions of tax jurisdiction and enforcement.

Chapter 8: Natural Resource Allocation and Management

- Much state-tribal litigation has occurred over water, timber, and fishing rights.

- Natural resources and the environment play a major role in tribal self-sufficiency as well as in tribal traditions and religion.

- Tribal water rights are significant, particularly in the West.

- Some tribes and states have negotiated and settled water rights questions rather than litigating them.

- Tribal treaty rights to fish and hunt have led to confrontations between Indian and non-Indian citizens.

- States and tribes have negotiated natural resource management arrangements as well as major land use settlements.

- Strong state and tribal leadership has promoted state-tribal agreements.

Chapter 9: Environmental Regulation

- Pollution does not respect political boundaries such as those that exist between state and tribal lands.

- Environmental protection is especially conducive to coordinated approaches and cooperative efforts of states and tribes.

- The U.S. Environmental Protection Agency treats tribes as states, although tribes have fewer financial resources than states.

- Many examples exist of state-tribal cooperative arrangements for environmental management.

- Hazardous materials transportation is emerging as a new area of state-tribal cooperation.

Chapter 10: Solutions for the 21st Century

- Congress should enact legislation to encourage states and tribes to enter into inter-governmental agreements for their mutual benefit.

- Congress should give high priority to funding the efforts contained in agreements resolved by states and tribes through negotiations.

- States should pass legislation allowing state agencies and political subdivisions to enter into intergovernmental agreements with Indian tribes.

- States should establish educational programs for state employees to expand their knowledge of tribal governments and Indian perspectives.

- Tribal and state leaders should try to work together to establish government-to-government relationships.

- Michigan and Montana offer valuable suggestions for improving state-tribal understanding.

1. THE NATIONS AMIDST THE STATES

In the old days before the white people came, people would talk until the issue was resolved. And if a decision wasn't ready to be made, that was okay. We're trying, in a modern sense, to continue the tradition of some Southwestern tribes that says, "Let's sit under a tree and talk. Let's share our food together. Let's reach a level of comfort so that we can, in a safe way, lay out our differences and begin to narrow those differences where possible, and define more precisely where our differences lie so that we can do more thinking and more information gathering around those differences. So the next time we talk, we can move the process further along."

– David Lester, Executive Director of the Council of Energy Resource Tribes

Interactions between states and Indian tribes across the United States are changing. In the 34 states where there are federally recognized Indian tribes, tribal governments are flexing their political and economic muscles and applying the principles of tribal sovereignty, self governance, and cultural and environmental preservation to endeavors that range from resource management to gambling to waste disposal. These activities bring focus and conflict to affairs between states and tribes and illustrate the need for more cooperative and mutually beneficial relations among these government entities. Some states with limited experience in the intricacies of Indian law and state-tribal relations have met legal and regulatory difficulties in dealing with tribes of which they were scarcely aware. Other states with longer histories of tribal-state dealings provide examples of cooperative agreements and enabling legislation for negotiation processes, commissions, committees, and special activities.

The state legislators who first came together in 1990 as the National Conference of State Legislatures' Task Force on State-Tribal Relations were concerned because serious disputes were under way between states and tribes from Florida to Washington and from Arizona to Wisconsin. Some of those disputes threatened the physical safety of participants. Yet it was also the "Year of Reconciliation" in South Dakota.

Legitimate differences exist between states and tribes, and the path to resolution of those differences is not drawn clearly. At the heart of state-tribal conflict is the question, "Who has the authority to do what?" The U.S. Constitution, in Article 1, Section 8, offers only this guidance: "The Congress shall have power . . . to regulate commerce with foreign nations, and among the several states, and with the Indian tribes." Over the years, evolving federal Indian policy has been expressed in treaties, executive orders, case law, federal statutes, federal regulations, and Congressional appropriations.

The treaties, executive orders, and agreements and statutes that established Indian reservations were vague with regard to the role of the states. In many cases where Indian treaties preceded statehood, the authority of state courts, revenue agencies, and wildlife departments has never been explicitly addressed. Without specific authority from Congress, states generally lack power over tribal members and their property on reservations, and they cannot interfere with tribal self-government, although Public Law 280, enacted in 1953, did give 15 states some jurisdiction in civil and criminal adjudication over Indians in their states. Generally however, tribal governments have the right to regulate their own members and their own lands, usually without interference by the states. This principle was reaffirmed by the U.S. Supreme Court in *Williams vs. Lee*, when the court stated that "absent governing acts of Congress, the question has always been whether the state action infringed on the right of reservation Indians to make their own laws and be ruled by them."

Clearly, the tribal relationship with the federal government has been dominant over that with the states. As states have learned through the years, federal Indian policy generally has supported the rights of Indian tribes to govern their people. Indian tribes and their governing councils possess inherent sovereign status with most of the requisite authority of self-governance and self-determination. Thus, states and tribes exist as mutual sovereigns, sharing contiguous geographic areas and common citizens.

States and tribes have been slow to accept one another as intergovernmental partners in the provision of services and in regulatory matters. This response may be due in part to past animosities and also to uncertainty about tribal regulatory and administrative capabilities.

Native American Indians

Rather than facing extinction, as many believe, the American Indian population is growing. Rising social and economic demands on tribal governments are forcing them to find new ways to respond and sometimes result in conflict between states and tribes over jurisdiction of gambling, taxation, waste disposal, natural resource use, and environmental regulation, as well as the provision of health, welfare, and education services.

When European explorers arrived in North America late in the 15th century, there were at least a million people already on the continent. Some estimates range as high as 15 million. They spoke more than 200 different languages in several unrelated linguistic families, according to the Center for Demographic Policy. Their political organizations ranged from highly sophisticated theocracies to small bands of hunter-gatherers.

By 1890, 400 years later, Native populations had sunk to less than half a million, decimated by European diseases and warfare. Today their numbers have grown again. In fact, 1990 census figures showed that 1.9 million people in the United States considered themselves to be American Indian, Inuit (Eskimo), or Aleut—0.8 percent of the total U.S. population. And there are approximately 200 languages and dialect groups within American Indian populations, in some cases known now by just a handful of people.

Native American people and their tribes still are so different from one another that referring to a monolithic "Indian community" seldom makes sense. Native Americans live in every state in the Union—in small towns, in villages, in big cities, on reservations, off reservations. Four states (all in the West) have Indian populations of 100,000 or more: Oklahoma, California, Arizona, and New Mexico. The six states where Natives make up 5 percent or more of the total population are Alaska, New Mexico, Oklahoma, South Dakota, Montana, and Arizona. Some of the most rapid population increases have taken place in Michigan, Texas, Florida, and Colorado. In addition, New England states (especially Maine) showed a major increase in American Indian populations during the seventies. Probably there is no single explanation for these increases, but a move toward greater awareness of and pride in one's racial and ethnic background during the last two decades may account for more people claiming Indian heritage and may account for some of the growth.

The Significance of Tribes

Tribes and tribal lands are extremely significant factors that affect the relationships of today's Native American people with other Americans and with state governments. There are more than 500 federally recognized tribes, some with tribal membership as small as 200, and one or two tribes having as many as 200,000 members. Today's tribal governments, at least superficially, are similar to other American political entities, but there are many variations.

Tribes enjoy the powers of governments, although their resources as governments differ from those of other governments. First, tribes as a general rule have not had the fiscal resources or the revenue base that states and local governments have had to support their activities. Consequently, tribes have been more dependent on federal financing for their programs. Second, most tribes are small in population and government structure, which has led to innovative solutions for governing and for providing services adapted to their needs and priorities.

In 1993, because of increased awareness of the concept of tribal sovereignty, President Clinton issued executive orders that included references to tribal governments as well as to state and local governments. The Environmental Protection Agency and the Department of Energy had developed formal policies in the early 1990s that addressed tribal governments as sovereign entities. The U.S. Advisory Commission on Intergovernmental Relations also acknowledged tribal governments in a 1993 report, and the federal mandate relief legislation signed by President Clinton in March 1995 refers to state, local, and tribal governments.

Tribes and Reservations

People sometimes use the terms "tribe" and "reservation" interchangeably when referring to an Indian government, but the two are not necessarily equivalent. Tribal governments existed long before "reservations" came into being, most within the past 130 years. Some 300 Indian reservations in the United States cover nearly 53 million acres of land in 32 states. They are called reservations because tribal leaders reserved for their tribes and their tribe's descendants certain homelands and certain rights when agreeing to give up other lands and activities. These reserved lands have shrunk over time for many reasons. Today, reservations range in size from the 15 million-acre Navajo reservation to the one-quarter-acre Golden Hill reservation in Connecticut.

Tribal governments exist off reservations as well as on reservations. In fact, there are some 30 tribal governments in Oklahoma, but considerably fewer reservations. Some tribes, such as the Shoshone and the Arapaho in Wyoming, share a reservation but have separate tribal governments. Some tribes reside on more than one reservation. This publication speaks of tribal governments as entities having responsibilities for self-governance, whether or not they have responsibilities for management of a specific area of land.

About half of the nation's Indian people reside on or near reservations. They are citizens of the United States and citizens of the states in which they live, with most of the same rights and responsibilities as any other citizen. Individual Native American Indians who are enrolled members of federally recognized tribes also are entitled to certain rights and benefits under federal laws based partly in early treaties and executive orders and partly in federal legislation that reaches back to the Dawes Act of 1887.

<table>
<tr><td>

Indian Country

Broadly speaking, Indian country is all the land under the supervision of the United States government that has been set aside primarily for the use of Indians. . . . The term "Indian Country" was first used by Congress in 1790 to describe the territory controlled by Indians. Today a federal statute concerning criminal jurisdiction provides the federal government's definition of this term. This law, Title 18, U.S. Code, section 1151,. . . identifies three areas as being "Indian country." First, Indian country includes all land within the boundaries of an Indian reservation, regardless of ownership. Thus, land located within a reservation but owned by a non-Indian is Indian country. Even rights-of-way through reservation lands, such as state or federal highways, remain a part of Indian country. Thus, whenever the federal government sets aside land under federal supervision for Indians, the land becomes Indian country. . . Second, Indian country includes "all dependent Indian communities" within the United States. A dependent Indian community is any area of land which has been set aside by the federal government for the use, occupancy or benefit of Indians, even if it is not a part of a reservation. The Pueblos of New Mexico, whose lands are owned by the tribes themselves but are under federal supervision, is an excellent example. . . . Finally, section 1151 includes as Indian country all "trust" and all "restricted" allotments of land, whether or not these allotments are inside an Indian reservation.

Reprinted from The Rights of Indians and Tribes: The Basic ACLU Guide to Indian and Tribal Rights by Stephen L. Pevar. Carbondale, Illinois: Southern Illinois University Press, 1992.

</td></tr>
</table>

Reservations have been called the "anchor tenants of rural America"; they are permanent fixtures that bring federal money into a region. Unlike military bases, however, they will never be shut down. One emerging realization for states with Indian reservations within their borders is that tribal economies can be contributors to a state's economy rather than a drain on it. For example, a recent study in Arizona found that tribes had a net positive impact of nearly $500 million on the state's economy. And Joe de la Cruz, former chairman of the Quinault Tribe in Washington, estimates a positive impact of $500 million by tribes on the Washington economy. Still, Indian people on reservations are among the most impoverished Americans. Some 60 percent of reservation families live below the poverty level, unemployment is high, and health problems abound.

The Significance of Treaties

European nations "treated" with the Indian nations as allies and equals during the wars of colonization. The U.S. government signed more than 400 treaties with Indian tribes, usually to gain rights to their lands. Many treaties were, in effect, real estate contracts. In exchange for lands and for agreement to cease resistance, tribes were promised protection, material goods, services, and sometimes cash payments.

A treaty is a legally binding contract between two sovereign nations that details the terms of an agreement between them. Article VI of the U.S. Constitution holds that treaties are "the supreme law of the land." Once a treaty is signed, both parties are bound to uphold the terms of agreement unless both parties consent to change these terms; the passage of time does not alter a treaty's validity. By entering into treaty agreements with Indian nations, the U.S. government acknowledged their sovereignty—their right to govern themselves within certain boundaries, to determine their membership, and to maintain their cultural and social integrity.

Treaty rights to hunt, fish, and gather wild rice or shellfish on ancestral lands and waters may accompany membership in some tribes. Rights to conduct certain economic activities—such as gambling—on Indian lands currently are protected under federal law. Native religious practices and sacred sites sometimes also receive protection under federal law. Indian people today who hold hunting and fishing rights do so because they are members of a certain tribe which has a treaty or an agreement with the federal government, not because they are ethnically Indian. In other words, their rights are political, not racial. Legal scholar Charles Wilkinson notes the present-day impact of treaties, saying that judges who have interpreted these long-ago promises have, in general, upheld the moral obligation of the promises against the "agonizingly powerful forces to abandon principle in the name of societal change."

What Is Tribal Sovereignty?

Indian tribes are inherently sovereign, meaning that they do not trace their existence to the United States, says Robert Laurence, law professor at the University of Arkansas in Fayetteville. In general, under the doctrine of inherent sovereignty, a tribe retains all governmental powers, absent an act of Congress. Treaties, the Constitution, and case law give Congress extensive power over tribal affairs. Nonetheless, according to *Federal Indian Law*, "Those powers which are lawfully vested in an Indian tribe are not, in general, delegated powers granted by express acts of Congress, but rather inherent powers of a limited sovereignty which has never been extinguished." According to the National Congress of American Indians, "Tribal leaders, like heads of other governments, thus may ponder whether any limitation exists to prevent them from acting in a particular manner, rather than whether any authority exists to permit their action."

Chief Justice John Marshall in 1831 characterized tribes as "domestic, dependent nations." William Canby writes that tribal sovereignty has these attributes:

- Indian tribes possess inherent governmental power over all internal affairs;
- The states are prevented from interfering with the tribes in their self-government; and
- Congress has plenary power to limit tribal sovereignty.

Since the treaty days, Congress and the federal court system have developed a body of so-called "Indian law" that over time has limited tribal sovereignty in some ways. But according to David Getches and Charles Wilkinson, the concept remains a vital force in state-tribal relations due to "its internal significance for tribal governments and the resulting external consequences for the states and non-Indian individuals and corporations within Indian Country."

State-Tribal Jurisdiction

Tribes are protective of their historical sovereignty and self-government. State leaders, on the other hand, usually assume that they have jurisdiction over any matter not granted specifically to the national government, as stated in the 10th Amendment to the U.S. Constitution: "The powers not delegated to the United States by the Constitution, nor prohibited by it to the States, are reserved to the States respectively, or to the people." According to a 1995 district court ruling in Rhode Island, "The extent to which state law applies in Indian Country is essentially one of accommodation between the interests of the tribes and the federal government on one hand and those of the state on the other." But, "State authority is also limited by tribal sovereignty and congressional power to regulate tribal affairs."

State-tribal jurisdictional questions may be framed in terms of territory, persons, subject matter, or a combination of these elements, according to the *Handbook on State-Tribal Relations.* There are categories in which the respective powers of states and tribes appear to be clearly established and exclusive, but there are also areas of ambiguity where exclusive jurisdiction in one or another government has not been established. Tribal-state conflict usually results from attempts of the governments to establish exclusive jurisdiction in ambiguous areas or to avoid responsibility.

Once the jurisdictional tension between state governments and tribal governments is acknowledged and its sources identified, the tension can be dealt with. States and tribes, as governments, can cooperate to assure adequate governmental service where jurisdiction is undefined. They also can try to coordinate policies and practices in areas of exclusive jurisdiction. Imagination and good will can go a long way toward improving state-tribal relations. Chapter 2 reports the results of a survey of state and tribal leaders that outlines their views on state-tribal relations and suggests ways to improve them.

References

Canby, William C. Jr. *American Indian Law in a Nutshell.* St. Paul, Minn.: West Publishing Co., 1988.

Center for Applied Research. *The Economic and Fiscal Importance of Indian Tribes in Arizona.* Denver, Colo.: Center for Applied Research, 1993.

Champagne, Duane. *Native America: Portrait of the Peoples.* Detroit: Visible Ink Press, 1994.

Commission on State Tribal Relations. *Handbook on State-Tribal Relations.* Albuquerque, N.M.: American Indian Law Center; and Denver, Colo.: National Conference of State Legislatures, 1983.

Council of Energy Resource Tribes. "Dialogue on Tribal Perceptions of the Ethical and Moral Bases of Nuclear Energy and Radioactive Waste Management." Transcript of a meeting of CERT, Colorado Springs, Colo., April 1992.

Deloria, Jr., Vine. *Behind the Trail of Broken Treaties.* New York: Dela Carte Press, 1974.

Getches, David H. "Negotiated Sovereignty: Intergovernmental Agreements with American Indian Tribes as Models for Expanding Self Government." *Review of Constitutional Studies* 1, no. 1 (1993).

Getches, David H. and Charles F. Wilkinson. *Federal Indian Law.* 2nd Edition. St. Paul, Minn.: West Publishing Co., 1986.

Laurence, Robert. American Indians and the Environment: A Legal Primer for Newcomers to the Field." *Natural Resources and Environment* 7, no. 4 (Spring 1993): 3-6; 48-50.

"Resource Management Plan Applicable to Indian Housing Project." *Narragansett Indian Tribe of Rhode Island v. Narragansett Electric Company et al.,* no. CA93-667T (D.R.I. Feb. 21, 1995). *National Environmental Enforcement Journal* 10, no. 7 (August 1995): 20-22.

Wilkinson, Charles F. *American Indians, Time and the Law.* New Haven: Yale University Press, 1987.

2. SURVEY OF STATE-TRIBAL RELATIONS

The NCSL Task Force on State-Tribal Relations conducted a survey in late 1991 and early 1992 to pinpoint areas for future research and assistance to states and tribes in their efforts to work together. The survey sought input on key state-tribal concerns and the extent of state-tribal cooperation. The survey showed that sovereignty is often at the core of disputes between state and tribal leaders. Although sovereignty invokes disagreements, the survey also suggests that there are more points of harmony than either side may think and that communication is the key to building a good working relationship between two governments.

Methodology

NCSL mailed a 16-question survey to House and Senate leadership of each state, to legislators with a particular interest in tribal affairs, to tribal leaders throughout the country, to tribal associations, and to state attorneys general. The results discussed here are based on 79 responses, representing 23 states and 34 Indian tribes: 22 responses from legislators, 41 from tribal officials, and 16 responses from attorneys general. States with large Native American populations are well represented. This chapter's discussion is based solely on the survey responses.

State-Tribal Communication

Tribes communicate their concerns about state policy issues to state governments in many ways: through the governor's office, the legislature, councils, special committees, or agencies. No one organizational structure appears to be superior, but several systems seem to work. The most important aspect of state-tribal communication is not which office handles Indian issues, but that Native Americans know the best place to take a particular concern, and that once there, it is dealt with in an understanding and educated manner.

Tribal leaders say that they communicate primarily with individual legislators or the governor's staff. Legislators cite the governor's office rather than their own body as the most common avenue of communication. Both groups also mention legislative committees, governors' commissions, tribal-state representatives, lobbyists, department heads, Indian liaisons within each agency, the attorney general's office, and state Indian offices as points of contact between tribal and state governments.

Virtually every survey respondent from a tribe has worked with members of the state legislature on state-tribal issues or other matters of concern to Native Americans in the state. Many states already have legislative committees, study groups, or interim committees in place to consider state-tribal issues. Almost all the state legislators mention that some such committee exists in their state, as well as a governor-appointed commission. Only half the tribal leaders note any type of state commission or committee dealing with tribal affairs, and they are less specific about whether it is legislative. This suggests a disparity between state and tribal leaders' perceptions as to what communications resources are available. Committees may exist, but unless they reach out to the tribal population and are receptive to tribal input, they are hampered in solving the issues critical to states and tribes.

State-Tribal Communication Lines Vary

A chairperson from a California tribe notes that her tribe has no established line of communication with the state and explains that when a major issue arises her tribe joins other tribes to openly demonstrate their opposition. This illustrates the importance of having some office, council, committee, or commission to facilitate state-tribal communication.

New Mexico's experience demonstrates that effective communication between committees and different branches of government is possible. Issues are identified by tribal governments and the Office of Indian Affairs. Common concerns are translated into policy statements adopted by the gubernatorially appointed New Mexico Commission on Indian Affairs. Policy and position papers are used to obtain support for action through the Legislative Indian Affairs Committee and state legislators. Legislation is discussed at joint sessions with the New Mexico Commission on Indian Affairs.

The Alabama Indian Affairs Commission is another example of a well-integrated effort. It is composed of 11 members, one from each of the seven tribes recognized by the state and one appointed by the governor, the lieutenant governor, the speaker of the House, and the commission, respectively. Representatives meet bimonthly or in special meetings. The commission can hold public hearings and can intervene in Indian issues and offer technical assistance.

Some tribes are part of intertribal councils or networks. A lobbyist for the Walker River Paiute Tribe explains that her tribe currently acts individually but is trying to build an intertribal organization that would act as a political action committee to increase the Indian political presence and coordinate efforts in dealing with the state and local governments. The state would benefit because it would be able to work with only one Native American group to address issues important to all member tribes.

A Summary of Critical Issues

States and tribes agree about the most important issues they face. The NCSL survey lists 19 issues: burial/reburial, child welfare, economic development, education, environmental protection, fishing, gambling, health services delivery, hunting, law enforcement, mining and minerals, religious freedom, sacred lands, sovereignty, taxation, timber/lumbering, urban Indians, waste transportation and disposal, and water rights.

State leaders cite economic development, gambling, sovereignty, education, and taxation (in that order) as the most pressing. They also list water rights, law enforcement, and health services, but with less frequency.

Tribal leaders give sovereignty and economic development equal billing as the two most crucial issues, closely followed by child welfare, education, gambling, and taxation (in that order). Law enforcement, fishing rights, environmental protection, and water rights are other concerns important to tribal leaders.

Though the NCSL survey asks leaders to identify the five most critical issues, many tribal leaders note that all the issues are important, and each has taken a position of prominence at one time or another. The deputy director of the Office of Indian Affairs in New Mexico explains that his office works on all the issues all the time because individual tribes have different priorities. The president of the Central Council of the Tlingit and Haida Indian Tribes of Alaska mentions native hiring in state government as another critical issue.

Furthermore, tribal leaders note that these topics are all interrelated. Economic development can't happen without education. The success of education programs is linked to good child welfare systems. Fair taxation agreements with the state encourage economic development on the reservation. As the tribal manager for the Cocopah Tribe in Arizona explains, gaming provides funds for tribes to improve education, social welfare, and additional economic development; thus, it has a very high priority. The tribal manager from the Grand Traverse Band of Ottawa and Chippewa Indians in Michigan also emphasizes the importance of gambling. He explains that the profits from gambling are crucial for funding education and social programs. Gambling profits fill a void created by funding cuts from the federal government.

State officials hold widely varying views about the suitability of gambling. A Washington state senator explains that it has recently become a critical issue because the agreement that allows tribal gambling enterprises overrides state law. He is concerned that this will lead to a deterioration of relations between the tribes and other citizens. A Florida official mentions the fear of increased crime associated with gaming. A Louisiana staffer says that gaming forces states to focus on the sovereignty of tribes.

Sovereignty

The recognition and exercise of sovereignty is the issue at the heart of many state-tribal disputes and agreements. More than half the tribal leaders report that their states have formally recognized tribal sovereignty. Such formal recognition has taken the form of a governor's proclamation, an act passed by the legislature (often both a proclamation and a law), occasionally a court decision, and sometimes federal involvement.

Formal recognition is not always a clear matter, however. The governor of Washington issued a proclamation of sovereignty, but the attorney general stated that it had no effect, according to one tribal leader. Likewise, in Alaska, according to tribal leaders, a previous governor granted sovereignty only to have it rescinded by a later governor. An Alaskan legislator explains that sovereignty has been granted to the one tribe that has a reservation but does not extend to the many other tribes that do not live under such an arrangement. A similar situation exists in Alabama and Utah, where the question "what is a tribe?" further complicates the already difficult sovereignty issue.

In addition, whether a state has formally recognized sovereignty is occasionally a matter of debate. Discrepancies appear among respondents from the same state about whether sovereignty has been recognized in their state and, if so, in what form and to what effect. One respondent from Minnesota notes that it had been recognized in a limited capacity by the federal courts, while another said that sovereignty was recognized by an act passed by the legislature. A third states that there was no formal recognition at all.

Many tribal leaders note that although their states have formally recognized tribal sovereignty, that status is neither acknowledged nor understood by many state officials. The revenue director for the Lake Traverse Band in Michigan illustrates this by explaining that his state consistently overrides tribal sovereignty by taxing economic development projects on Indian land claiming "realty improvements." Tribal residents of Washington note that, although they have relatively good relations with the state, the state legislature passed a growth management act that did not provide a mechanism for tribes to participate as governments, leading to conflicts with county governments.

Collaboration also occurs with local governments. A tribal authority for the Barona Band of Mission Indians in California explains that there is a more cooperative relationship with the county government than with the state. He attributes this to the fact that the county is "using federal funds to staff and support a special Indian liaison task force which is providing a better level of service than before." The county does not assert direct regulatory jurisdiction but works with the reservation to present recommendations not demands. In contrast, he feels that the state's attitude is largely to refuse to acknowledge the tribe's sovereignty and to insist on enforcing state law. For instance the California Integrated Waste Management Board has demanded that the tribe submit to state regulation of used tire disposal on the reservation. The tribal council refused to submit to state regulatory jurisdiction that they feel does not apply to them, but offered to discuss voluntary cooperation.

Such anecdotal evidence suggests that cooperation is more feasible when tribes are asked to participate in solution-oriented discussions rather than being expected to adhere to state demands concerning jurisdiction. Sovereignty can be respected to the mutual benefit of states and tribes.

Dispute Resolution

States and tribes use several methods to settle their differences. State leaders mention joint efforts between tribes and state agencies as a popular method. They also note cooperative agreements, litigation, and negotiation as ways often used to solve problems. Tribes cite litigation as the foremost method used, although they also mention negotiation, joint efforts between tribes and state agencies, and informal working agreements. Unfortunately, both sides tend toward the use of litigation to resolve differences. This approach is time-consuming and costly for all concerned, without promoting a deeper understanding of each other's problems and needs.

Regardless of how a dispute is resolved, both tribal and state leaders agree that a written document is necessary in virtually all cases. Both groups feel that a document promotes better understanding of the agreement, improves communication and encourages a government-to-government approach (particularly important to tribal leaders). A written document is especially important because it helps eliminate any differences in administration and implementation. A state official notes that, since issues usually arise out of the unique legal status of the tribes, the legal rights of both parties should be spelled out in the language of a contract. Furthermore, once on paper, the agreement is binding even though leadership on either side may change.

There is some disagreement between states and tribes about who should participate in the process that leads to a written document. Everyone agrees that the tribal chief, chairman, or governor and the tribal council should represent the Indian concerns. However, state representation is more complex. Legislators tend to suggest that it should include tribal leadership and officials from state agencies, the attorney general's office, and the governor's office, or their delegates. Many feel that legislators should be involved and that some agreements should be ratified by the legislature.

Tribal representatives strongly believe that in order to promote a government-to-government relationship, officials of comparable status should be involved in a dispute resolution process. They are concerned that state agency officials often do not have the authority to back up their side of an agreement. Many tribal leaders say they prefer to deal directly with the governor of their state; none mention the legislature. However, they do suggest the presence of an informed but disinterested party who could help mediate negotiations. Both state and tribal respondents agree that high-ranking government officials from each side, including the governor and the tribal chair, should sign the final agreement. Some respondents from both groups suggest that any agreement should be backed by a resolution of the state legislative bodies.

Successful State-Tribal Agreements

While respondents cite dozens of state-tribal agreements, opinions vary about which agreements are successful; some are water agreements, cross-deputization, land settlements, and the formation of Indian-related committees. One-quarter of the tribal leaders state that no agreements beneficial to Indians have been reached. However, the remaining tribal respondents speak enthusiastically about state-tribal programs such as cross-deputization, child welfare, foster care, hunting and fishing agreements, tax sharing, public safety, mutual assistance, and gambling. Respondents mention the following successful agreements:

Law Enforcement

- A mutual law enforcement assistance agreement in Michigan that authorizes cross-deputization of law enforcement officers on the reservation, joint dispatching, and dispute resolution.

- A Cherokee Nation arrangement with the county sheriff's offices that involves payments to assist in defraying costs of handling Indian prisoners, warrants, and other court-related costs.

- Similar law enforcement agreements are in place in at least seven other states.

Taxes

- Tax refund/rebate agreements (including gasoline) that the Michigan Department of Treasury negotiated with each tribe in 1977-78 have been renewed annually.

- A tax sharing agreement between South Dakota and the Oglala Sioux tribe.

- Nevada, North Carolina, and Wisconsin have tax agreements with adjacent tribes.

Foster care and child protection

- Tribal foster care services in Montana, whereby the state agreed that one tribe would establish its own foster care licensing procedures and license foster homes, and the state would cover the payments.

- In Michigan, emergency protective services agreements between county departments of social services negotiated in the early 1980s.

- Survey respondents note agreements in Oklahoma, South Dakota, Wisconsin, and Wyoming.

Land claims

- The Washington State/Puyallup Tribe land claims agreement that took into account a number of interests.

- Agreements on land claims were also reached in Connecticut, Florida, Maine, and New York.

Additional examples

- In Oklahoma, a Department on Tourism-initiated annual conference on tourism is held in collaboration with tribal governments; and the Oklahoma Supreme Court sponsors an annual conference on tribal sovereignty.

- Hunting, fishing, and wildlife accords have been reached in Alaska, Idaho, Maine, Michigan, Minnesota, Montana, Nevada, Washington, and Wisconsin.

- Legislation authorizing intergovernmental agreements has been enacted in Minnesota, New Mexico, and Washington.

- Reburial is addressed by Maryland and North Dakota agreements.

- Idaho and Montana have negotiated water rights compacts with bordering Indian nations.

- An annual reception put on by Native Americans at the state capitol in Maine to encourage interaction between tribal members and legislators.

- Other accords deal with revenue sharing (Maine), solid waste (Arizona and North Carolina), housing (Minnesota), education (Minnesota), traffic (Michigan and North Dakota), energy assistance (North Carolina), and water pollution (New York).

Increased Communication and Education as the Keys

All the respondents stress that an open-door relationship between tribal and state governments contributes to successful agreements and to positive relations in general. They also suggest ways to create or enhance meaningful communication.

Both state and tribal leaders mention the formation of a state-tribal relations or Indian affairs committee as helping to promote communication. State leaders feel that Native Americans working in state government positions help to improve relations.

A Minnesota state senator suggests that legislators listen to suggestions from Indian people and act on those recommendations. A senator from Oklahoma suggests that legislators work with the governor's office to establish legislative policy designed to improve state tribal relations, but fears that bureaucratic state agencies might prove to be obstacles.

A state official from Oregon notes: "Any program that joins tribal representatives and state officials is valuable. There needs to be a positive climate in which state officials can learn to understand and appreciate their responsibilities in light of the unique legal rights possessed by their Indian citizens." This statement underlines the value of committee work—bringing people from different perspectives together to talk about the issues that affect them all.

Tribal government officials view sovereignty as the key issue that must be resolved in order to improve relations, while state government officials rarely mention tribal sovereignty as a point on which to improve understanding. This difference presents an obstacle that tribal representatives believe is the result of ignorance on the part of state officials about Indian law, treaty rights, and culture. As a leader of the Penobscot Indian Nation comments, "State-tribal relations are based on a warped history, without regard to the truths espoused within the Constitution. Treaties are constitutional, yet no school studies the Indian treaties. State legislators are the product of this educational system that evades the truth of Indian history. There is a tendency to categorize Native Americans as 'just another minority group,' without understanding the intricate history of tribal agreements with the federal and state governments."

Leaders also note paternalism, fear, and a pervasive history of misunderstanding as stumbling blocks to attempted improvements in state-tribal relations. They cite a need to redefine historical texts so that non-Indians learn that Indian tribes and people are not obscure relics and that tribes and states need not automatically be on opposing sides of every issue. One tribal leader stressed, "We just need more honest effort."

A tribal-state representative from Maine suggests the formation of a Native American office at the state government level. The chairman of the Stockbridge Munsee Band of Mohicans (Wisconsin) recommends that a person chosen by tribal governments should fill a position (to be created) at the "Indian desk" in the governor's office.

Both sides agree that two-way communication and education are the keys to conquering these problems, and all emphasize the importance of face-to-face meetings, such as annual conferences. Leaders also suggest newsletters about Native American affairs, educational workshops for state employees, and Native American cultural events as ways to improve understanding and communication between tribal and state governments. Relationships between state and tribal officials need to be cultivated at other levels of government as well.

Potential Collaboration

Improved communication and understanding pave the way for collaborative action that benefits both states and tribes. Both state and tribal leaders single out a variety of issues they view as suitable for cooperative efforts; these differ from state to state.

- *Economic development.* Tribes are permanent residents of a state, and unlike many businesses, they won't leave when they find a cheaper lease or better tax deal elsewhere.

- *Environmental protection and resource management.* Some states acknowledge that tribes have developed technical expertise in these areas and are ready to tap into their talent.

- *Child welfare, law enforcement, public safety, and education.* Tribes should participate in any reforms that might enable these systems to be more responsive to tribal and local needs.

- *Gambling.* Gambling is a potential area for cooperation because it is a good source of revenue for tribes while providing benefits to the larger community. A senator from Washington observes that having the tribes run casinos helps structure what could otherwise be an unmanageable industry.

The Tough Issues

Sovereignty and its jurisdictional conflicts lie at the core of issues like taxation, gambling regulation, and land rights. These issues bring up the touchy topics that government officials from both sides usually prefer to avoid.

Some state officials see tribal members being granted rights superior to other citizens and feel that this inequality was not the intention of treaties. A Washington senator notes, "Equal rights for all citizens is the only long-range, workable formula."

Some tribal leaders believe that they have made efforts to reach out to state officials only to have their advances snubbed. State governments play a crucial role in tribal issues, but many state government workers see tribal concerns as just one of many competing issues that crowd their desks.

Actions for a Positive Future

The survey shows that state-tribal relations are far more advanced in some states than in others. Why? Respondents suggest that state and tribal governments that work together on less controversial issues learn about each other in the process. Collaboration demands a willingness to overlook what might seem to be glaring differences in order to search for common ground. Increased understanding and communication that results from cooperation on less demanding issues fosters an improved ability to work together in the future. Success is not so closely related to what type of state organization, office, or committee has been set up to deal with tribal issues as it is a function of (1) how involved Native Americans are in the political structure, (2) how good the communication is between different branches of government dealing with Indian affairs, (3) how good the communication is between state government offices and Native American communities, and (4) how much the employees of those offices understand and care about state-tribal relations.

3. SEEKING COMMON GROUND THROUGH STATE-TRIBAL AGREEMENTS

This chapter continues the discussion begun in Chapter 2 about ways that states and tribes try to resolve their differences. The two approaches used most often are litigation and negotiations that result in agreements.

The NCSL task force began its work already focused on the idea of state-tribal agreements to help resolve jurisdictional questions, primarily because of earlier work done by the Commission on State-Tribal Relations. The commission was formed in 1977 by tribal leaders, legislators, governors, and county commissioners who were interested in improving the interactions of states and tribes. It produced the *Handbook on State-Tribal Relations* and *State-Tribal Agreements: A Comprehensive Study*.

Members of the 1990 NCSL task force drew upon those works for guidance. Their discussions also frequently echoed author Vine DeLoria, writing in *Behind the Trail of Broken Treaties*, "The responsibility of any nation and the particular responsibility of elected officials of any nation is not to justify what has passed for legality but to anticipate the conditions and problems of tomorrow and attempt to deal with them."

Talks and educational sessions around the topic of state-tribal relations sparked new perspectives. Awareness grew that state-tribal relations offer the possibility of engaging in an approach that Ted Gaebler and David Osborne call "anticipating government." Rather than being "future-blind," and reacting to one crisis after another, "anticipating governments" do two things: "They use an ounce of prevention, rather than a pound of cure; and they do everything possible to build foresight into this decision making."

How does this process start? Reinventing government is a long-term effort. Anthropologist Bea Medicine, a member of the Lakota tribe, uses the Lakota term *washichu* to refer to white people. Literally, it means "he reaches for all things." Another translation is "capricious spirits." The legacy of capricious actions toward Indian people will not be overcome quickly, but much can take place in present and future relationships between states and tribes to honor cultural diversity and base future policies on consensual outcomes and compassion for the human condition.

Applying the "anticipating government" idea to state-tribal relations might mean that state legislatures should recognize tribes as intergovernmental partners whose cultural, religious, environmental, and economic health is tied to that of non-Indian society. For tribes, it might mean recognizing the incentives that drive state decision makers and striving to find the common interests that bring different constituencies together. Working out a collective vision of the future would be the outcome. The tribes that plan their actions thinking of the effect on the next seven generations already take the long view. Both states and tribes must overcome the past by looking to the future.

Responsibilities of Governments

Tribes and states, as governments, provide services that see to the protection, health, education, and welfare of their citizens. The responsibilities of government cannot be ignored, so disputes must be resolved, legal questions answered, and relationships proceed. Tension arises out of differences over the best ways to accomplish those responsibilities, particularly around the issue of whose rules apply in a given situation and which government will pay for solutions. This "sorting out" of governmental responsibilities is an ongoing process at all governmental levels.

Negotiated Settlements

Dispute resolution through negotiation offers states and tribes an alternative to litigation. One type of negotiation process begins as an open-ended and relatively unfocused discussion of the intergovernmental relationship that later narrows to a discussion of specific coordination issues. Another focuses from the outset on a single issue or specific agenda of issues. Results of negotiation processes may be as formal as a written settlement signed by the state governor and tribal chairman and approved by Congress, or as simple as a handshake between state and tribal officials responsible for implementing certain regulations. The Indian Reorganization Act of 1934 specifically states that tribes that accept its provisions have the power to negotiate with state and municipal governments. It also may be advisable to keep appropriate federal officials involved with the progress of negotiations, particularly if the national government is expected to assume part of the financial burden for implementing an agreement, or if federal policy must be coordinated with tribal and state policies.

In addressing the topic of negotiating state-tribal jurisdictional issues, Regis Pecos, executive director of the New Mexico Office of Indian Affairs, has recognized the benefits of negotiation:

> While this form of resolution is not universally accepted by the tribes or the states, most responsible tribal and state governments have been open to exploring the possibilities presented by negotiated settlements of jurisdictional disputes. . . . Each agreement will have to be carefully tailored to address the specific situation to which it relates. For much the same reason, the advisability of comprehensive [federal] legislation to address such matters is doubtful. . . .[C]omprehensive legislation lacks the ability to address the special circumstances that exist in different areas of the country. For example, in the state of Montana, virtually all of the reservations have been open to non-Indian settlement. As a result these reservations have large non-Indian populations and significant non-Indian land ownership within the reservations. In this circumstance, the interests of the state clearly are greater than in the case of New Mexico, where lands within the reservations generally are owned by the tribes and few non-Indians reside within the reservations. The solution to jurisdiction problems that work in New Mexico will not work in Montana. Each state, therefore, should resist federal legislation that would limit its options in dealing with tribal governments.

One of the most promising areas for use of negotiation is in resolving western tribal water rights claims. Previous Indian water rights cases that have been litigated have proved to be very lengthy and expensive to all parties and ultimately do not resolve all of the water-related issues among the parties. (For additional detail, see chapter 8.) As a result, an increasing number of tribes, states, non-Indian water users, and federal officials are resorting to negotiations to find solutions. Recently, Indian water rights settlements have been negotiated by the Colorado Utes, Salt River Pima-Maricopas in Arizona, Idaho's Fort Hall Shoshone-Bannocks, the Northern Cheyenne in Montana, and the Seminole Tribe of Florida. Congress has approved most of those settlements and appropriated funds to help implement them.

Achieving a settlement through negotiation requires tremendous commitment from the parties involved. Mediation, facilitation, and other forms of assisted negotiation can offer innovative, cost-effective, and comprehensive methods to help resolve disputes. Looking to a neutral party for assistance in resolving disputes is a long-standing tradition in many Indian nations. The Navajo and the Hopi, for example, have always had a "headsman," the person to whom disputing parties bring their complaints. History has created a vast gulf between Indian and non-Indian societies, and the bridge across can be hard to walk, but the search for peaceful solutions and for consensus that serves all interests is solidly based in many tribal cultures.

Intergovernmental Agreements and Compacts

The result of negotiation and a key mechanism for shared governing is the intergovernmental agreement between a tribe and a state or local government entity. Such an agreement "can give practical meaning to broad legal concepts," according to University of Colorado law professor David H. Getches. "At a minimum such agreements clarify ambiguous laws. They can close the space between legal concepts of sovereignty and the practical necessities of governing. In some cases they can resolve disputes that would otherwise be mired in costly, protracted, and sometimes inconclusive litigation."

States, tribes, and local governments have negotiated hundreds of such intergovernmental agreements, 150 in the area of gaming alone (see chapter 6). These numbers indicate that pragmatic negotiation can often overcome legal uncertainty, but equally important is enforcement of agreements. Both sides must honor the principles contained within agreements; otherwise, future negotiations are devalued. Agreements that are working include the following examples.

Puyallup Tribal Settlement. In the early 1980s, the Port Authority and City of Tacoma, Washington, realized they were losing their court challenges against the Puyallup Tribe regarding jurisdiction over more than 20,000 acres of urban and industrialized land. With the involvement of state, tribal, federal, and local officials and the assistance of mediators, a negotiated settlement was signed in March 1990. The settlement package totaled $162 million, and provided over $111 million in direct benefits to the Puyallup Tribe and its members. The federal government agreed to provide $77.3 million (48 percent), the state $21 million (13 percent), local governments $52.1 million (32 percent), and private contributors $11.5 million (7 percent). The Puyallup Tribe gave up its claim to all but 900 acres in exchange for the money—$20,000 cash for each tribal member; a $22 million social, health, and welfare trust fund; a $3.5 million jobs program with local businesses; and $51 million for dredging and road improvements on the tribe's reserved acreage along the waterfront.

Wisconsin and Ojibwe (Chippewa) Tribes. These tribes have reached two deer-hunting agreements, two trapping agreements, two ice-fishing agreements, and agreements on open-water fishing, wild rice harvesting, and small game hunting. The agreements have resulted in no adverse impact on the resources, have protected public safety, and have addressed the social and economic concerns of northern Wisconsin. The agreements have allowed the exercise of Chippewa federally supported treaty rights to hunt, fish, and gather on a portion of the 16 million acres they gave to the U.S. government in 1837 and 1842.

Idaho and the Coeur d'Alene Tribe. The state and the tribe in 1988 signed an agreement regarding tribal members' rights to off-reservation hunting, fishing, and trapping in ceded lands.

Tribes and State Legislatures: Working Together

State legislatures also are an increasingly important forum for the discussion and resolution of state-tribal relations, most particularly in states with significant populations of Indian citizens. As one alternative to the judicial system, the state political process has the potential to produce outcomes more agreeable to all parties than can the adversarial courts.

Non-Indians frequently are unfamiliar with the demands on tribal governments, with the history and implications of federal Indian law, and with the perspectives of Indian constituents. The legislative process offers an opportunity for Indians and non-Indians alike to learn more about each other. Finding a path in the two political worlds of states and tribes can be a real challenge. In 10 states at least 30 Native American legislators currently balance their membership in a sovereign tribe with service as an elected state official. Their concerns are not restricted exclusively to so-called Indian issues. Indian people want most of the same things that any other people want: good schools, adequate health care, good roads, and comfortable housing. But because of tribal relationships with the federal government and the historic prohibition on state government involvement with tribal matters, the needs of Indian people sometimes slip through the cracks. Indian legislators work at the state level to ensure that Indian citizens are not forgotten in the state political process.

In the state legislative sessions from 1991 to 1995, nearly 1,500 pieces of legislation were introduced that concerned issues of state-tribal relations. In 1995, 467 bills were introduced, of which 71 were enacted and 90 were pending. In 1991 220 bills were introduced with 77 enactments. The trend is toward an ever-increasing number of bills and resolutions being brought for consideration to state legislative bodies with a consequently greater number of enactments. The majority of this legislation was sponsored by Native legislators.

A variety of issues has been addressed in the state legislatures. Over the five-year period 1991-1995, the issue having the most enactments (45) dealt with Native American committees and organizations. The next was education with 30 enactments, health (21), gaming (19), Native American holidays and ceremonials (14), and land claims (14). Other issues that affect Indians addressed by state legislation are taxation, natural resource allocation and protection (hunting, fish, timber, water), burial protection, authority for intergovernmental agreements, economic development, cultural and historical preservation, waste disposal, sovereignty recognition, religious freedom, tribal courts, and child welfare. It is clear that as Indian people become more involved in state politics, their visibility will increase, enhancing the visibility of the political issues that are important to them.

Litigation

Finally, litigation also has a useful place in state-tribal relations. Under some circumstances, lawsuits are more suitable than working out differences in other ways. Courts can clarify murky jurisdictional questions. When a question of law remains unclear, the courts, especially the U.S. Supreme Court, can make a statement that is heard across the land. In situations that pit non-Indian citizens against Indian citizens over hunting and fishing, taxes, gambling, and other treaty rights that appear to treat Indians as "special," legal decisions can protect elected public officials from having to take a stand on inflammatory issues. For example, some voters demanded the recall of a Wisconsin legislator because they considered his position as too "pro-Indian." The recall election kept him in office, but the turmoil called attention to the strong attitudes and emotions surrounding state-tribal issues. Courts can provide the final word in these cases.

Litigation has negative aspects as well, however. Perhaps the major objection to litigation is that a court decision always results in a winner and a loser, causing resentment and likely future trouble. A second objection is that most court decisions often can be applied only to very specific situations, leaving many related questions unanswered and subject to further litigation. Third, court decisions are seldom predictable, encouraging ongoing lawsuits. Fourth, court decisions usually do not acknowledge the specialized needs of people, focusing instead on points of law. And last, litigation is expensive. States and tribes often could do better than to spend their funds on lawsuits.

Seeking Common Ground

Several factors in the 1990s place greater demands on state and tribal governments to work out their differences. These factors include increased willingness by the U.S. Congress to delegate to Indian tribes regulatory and implementation functions previously accorded only to states; a Supreme Court less predictable on tribal self-determination; and a growing movement on the part of Indian nations to preserve their heritage, exercise self-governance, and define the legitimate functions of a sovereign governmental entity. The potential changes for Indian nations represented by the administration of President Bill Clinton and the Republican-dominated Congress will intensify tribes' focus on the nation's capital. But states, as "laboratories of democracy," are involved in the day-to-day innovations that shape the practical realities of shared governing, and Indian nations may find it prudent to negotiate with the states when possible. Federal budget cuts increase the need for cooperation in allocating scarce financial resources.

For state and tribal governments to work at cooperation and coordination of their policies, willingness to negotiate must exist on both sides. Whether that willingness is there will depend on the personalities involved, past history, legal conditions, the opportunity for real achievements, and the issues at stake. The complexity of state-tribal disputes can be daunting. The number and diversity of tribes and the differences among states create an intricate mosaic of issues to be dealt with. The theme of tribal sovereignty runs through it all, and the stakes are high. Browning Pipestem, tribal judge and professor of law, has called tribal sovereignty the "last plane out of Casablanca—the best chance for tribes to find a way out of poverty and despair." Tribes will fight against attempts to limit or eliminate tribal sovereignty. States will need to recognize the importance of sovereignty as the base for tribal movement forward in efforts to improve the lives of Indian citizens.

The traditions and history of tribal governments, and the changes with which they are coping today, greatly affect state-tribal interactions. Government officials—tribal, state, and local—who understand these complications are better prepared to work out intergovernmental arrangements to solve them than officials who are unfamiliar with such situations. Beginning with chapter 4, this publication examines some of today's most pressing state-tribal issues with emphasis on state-tribal cooperative approaches.

References

Commission on State Tribal Relations. *Handbook on State-Tribal Relations.* Albuquerque, N.M.: American Indian Law Center; and Denver, Colo.: National Conference of State Legislatures, 1983.

Deloria, Jr., Vine. *Behind the Trail of Broken Treaties.* New York: Dela Carte Press, 1974.

Hodgkinson, Harold L. *The Demographics of American Indians.* Washington, D.C.: Center for Demographic Policy, Institute for Educational Leadership, Inc., 1990.

Flynn, Janet, and Scott Ratliff (project director). *Tribal Government: Wind River Reservation.* Riverton, Wyo.: Big Bend Press, 1991.

Getches, David H. "Negotiated Sovereignty: Intergovernmental Agreements with American Indian Tribes as Models for Expanding Self Government." *Review of Constitutional Studies* 1, no. 1 (1993).

Jacquez, Melinda. *1995 State Legislation on Native American Issues.* Denver: National Conference of State Legislatures, October 1995.

Lincoln, Kenneth, *The Good Red Road.* New York: Harper & Row, 1987.

McGaa, Ed. *Native Wisdom: Perceptions of the Natural Way.* Minneapolis: Four Directions Publishing, 1995.

Morin, Kimberly A. *1994 State Legislation on Native American Issues.* Denver: National Conference of State Legislatures, September 1994.

Nabokov, Peter. *Native American Testimony.* New York: Penguin Group, 1978, 1991.

Neihardt, John G. *Black Elk Speaks.* Lincoln: University of Nebraska, 1961.

Osborne, David, and Ted Gaebler. *Reinventing Government.* Reading, Mass.: Addison-Wesley, 1992.

Pecos, Regis. Memorandum to Governor Bruce King, "Briefing Paper on State/Tribal Issues." May 6, 1991.

Pipestem, Browning. Presentation on Sovereignty at National Conference of State Legislatures' Annual Meeting, Nashville, Tenn., Aug. 6, 1990.

Reed, James B. "1991 State Legislation Relating to Native Americans." *State Legislative Report* (National Conference of State Legislatures) 16, no. 9 (December 1991).

Reed, James B. "Notes from National Congress of American Indians Tribal Seminar on Nuclear Waste," September 11-13, 1989, Phoenix, Ariz. Photocopied.

Steiner, Stan. *The Vanishing White Man.* New York: Harper & Row, 1976.

White-Tail Feather, Alex; James B. Reed; and July Zelio. *State-Tribal Legislation: 1992 and 1993 Summaries.* Denver: National Conference of State Legislatures, 1994.

Zelio, Judy A. "Indian Legislators Break New Ground," *State Legislatures* 18, no. 3, (March 1992): 18-20.

4. STATE ROLES IN INDIAN HEALTH, EDUCATION, AND CHILD WELFARE

Health, education, and child welfare offer states and Indian tribes significant potential to work together, although that potential has not been fully realized in most places. For instance, many non-Indians assume that Native Americans receive their health care exclusively from the federal Indian Health Service. Actually, state and local governments play major roles in providing health services to many Indian people. State and local governments also are the primary educators of Indian young people, and they play a significant part in the placement of Indian children in appropriate homes when parents cannot care for them. This chapter highlights the state-tribal relationships that generally prevail in these three policy areas.

Health

The national government historically has designed, paid for and supervised Indian health programs. The federal Indian Health Service (IHS), part of the Public Health Service, is the primary care provider for tribal members who live on or near reservations. Many who live outside Indian country, however, do not have access to direct IHS services or IHS-supported urban clinics, even though they qualify for the services.

Statistics indicate that the health of Indian people improved between 1980 and 1990. However, their life expectancy is still behind that of the U.S. population as a whole. Diseases of the heart are the leading cause of death for Indian people and injuries are second. The risk of motor-vehicle-related death is nearly three times greater for Indians than for the population as a whole.

Alcohol-related illness affects all Indian age groups, and young people are at high risk. The U.S. House of Representatives Select Committee on Children, Youth and Families has reported that by 12th grade one boy in four is a problem drinker. The death rate from suicide for Indian adolescents is 2.6 times that of other ethnic groups; 80 percent of suicides are alcohol-related. Fetal alcohol syndrome continues to be a serious problem.

Ear infections constitute the major illness of Indian children. The resultant hearing loss affects language skills among children and adolescents. American Indians are especially vulnerable to diabetes mellitus. Diabetes currently is the second leading cause of adult outpatient visits in the IHS; and half of all adults in some Southwest tribes are reported to have the disease, the highest reported prevalence in the world. Risk factors include obesity, poor nutrition, and noncompliance with treatment.

HIV/AIDS is an increasing problem. According to the Centers for Disease Control and Prevention, between 1989 and 1990 the rate of AIDS cases among American Indians and Alaskan Natives increased faster than among any other ethnic or racial group in the United States. To increase awareness of these issues, in 1993, the NCSL, with support from the American Foundation for AIDS Research, the Centers for Disease Control and Prevention, and the Burroughs Wellcome Company, brought together state legislators, tribal representatives, and state health officials from 10 states for a conference on HIV/AIDS promoting collaboration among health agencies, legislatures, and tribes to improve HIV prevention for Native American young people. The conference was successful in increasing awareness about HIV and Native American young people, and highlighted the need for greater state-tribal communication on this issue.

The conference also demonstrated that the belief that the federal government is responsible for all Indian health care is pervasive. This mistaken attitude can lead to leaving tribal governments out of the process of state planning and resource allocation, with the result that very little state legislation exists concerning Indian health care. Opportunities exist for states and tribes to cooperate to improve health care for Native Americans. Some states' efforts to address Indian health care issues are discussed below.

Arizona. In 1989 Arizona established an advisory council on Indian health care. Its purposes include developing a comprehensive health care delivery and financing system for American Indians specific to each Arizona tribe; facilitating communication and planning among tribes, the state, and federal agencies; and recommending Indian health care policies and legislation (A.R.S. § 36-2902.01-.02, passed 1988, amended 1989).

California. In 1983, California defined a program for American Indians and their families that includes studies of available health services; technical and financial assistance to local agencies; and coordination with similar programs of the federal government, other states, and voluntary agencies (Cal. Health & Safety Code § 1182).

To learn how to modify and improve health promotion and prevention services for minority groups in the state, the California Health Promotions Section in 1990 organized a steering committee from four major ethnic groups—African-American, Hispanic, Native American, and Asian/Pacific Islander. The committee established ethnic-specific task forces charged with prioritizing 10 issues and preparing discussion papers on four of them. The American Indian discussion papers covered nutrition, diabetes, cancer, and heart disease. Fifteen projects were funded, including two American Indian rural-based programs.

California Proposition 99 increased the state tobacco tax and directed that 20 percent of the proceeds be used for health education and tobacco use prevention. In 1991, the Tobacco Control Section established four ethnic networks to deal primarily with tobacco issues but also with other substances and cultural and family interactions. The American Indian network contracts with the California Rural Indian Health Board as facilitator of the networks. The network now involves approximately 30 agencies, including clinics, Indian volunteer groups, and some county health departments. Because of ceremonial uses of tobacco, tobacco prevention messages have had to be culturally sensitive and emphasize restricting tobacco to traditional uses rather than urging its complete elimination.

In 1991, the state required its Department of Health Services to improve the validity of American Indian death rate statistics and to identify ways to improve the quality of statistics when funds are appropriated.

Michigan. The Office of Minority Health in Michigan was first funded by legislation in 1988 to address the needs of five minority group populations. Programs relevant to American Indians include collaborative efforts with various statewide health and special group coalitions such as the Diabetes Education Coalition and the Minority Health Coalition; collaboration with other state departments and agencies via the Interagency Minority Health Coalition; and minority health professionals' support for careers in public health.

Minnesota. The Indian Health Board of Minneapolis (IHB), established in 1971, was the first urban Indian health program developed by local Indians to meet their needs. Funds for these services come from a large number of federal, state, county and local governmental, and private sources. In 1991-92, the IHS provided about 37 percent of the $3.37 million budget with direct service, substance abuse, and mental health funds. Patient revenues, including Medicare and Medicaid, contributed 16 percent, the Urban Health Initiative (U.S. Department of Health and Human Services) 12 percent, United Way 6.5 percent, the state Department of Health and Human Services 6 percent, and the W.K. Kellogg Foundation 3.5 percent. The remaining 19 percent of revenues came from 39 other sources.

The IHB administers a wide-ranging program of health-related services to urban Native Americans. In 1991, 82 percent of the 8,000 patients were Native Americans, representing 69 federally recognized tribes. The IHB began a dental clinic in 1972 and a medical clinic in 1974. Health education programs include family planning, prenatal care, diabetes planning, and one of Minneapolis' largest Women, Infants and Children's Programs. Patients needing hospitalization are referred to local facilities.

In 1991, the IHB reorganized its youth program to help American Indian youth develop the skills to make healthy life choices. The program focuses on chemical (substance abuse) awareness, development of self-esteem, academic achievement, cultural identity, and physical well-being.

Indian Mortality Rates Compared With Rates for U.S. All Races (Reservation States, Age-adjusted, 1988)	
Alcoholism	438 percent greater
Tuberculosis	400 percent greater
Diabetes mellitus	155 percent greater
Accidents	131 percent greater
Homicide	57 percent greater*
Pneumonia and influenza	32 percent greater
Suicide	27 percent greater

*The homicide rate is especially high among young males

Source: Indian Health Service, *Trends in Indian Health 1991*

North Dakota. The University of North Dakota School of Medicine educates a large proportion of the American Indian physicians in the United States. It is one of five Centers for Excellence in Health Care named by the federal Department of Health and Human Services for its training of Native American health care professionals. The federally funded Indians Into Medicine program supports the education of American Indians in each medical school class. In 1992, seven of 52 residents in the four family practice residency programs were Indian. In addition, the Department of Family Medicine offers a program that actively involves tribal leaders in educating tribal members about AIDS. Each year tribal councils select five leaders from each of the five North Dakota reservations to attend two four-day conferences. The program, funded by Bush/Northwest Foundations, focuses on AIDS awareness, education, and prevention. Participants receive $2,000 mini-grants to provide community-based HIV/AIDS education programs for their tribes.

Utah. In 1982, Utah's health department planning office found that members of minority groups suffered illnesses more often and had a higher mortality rate than the general population. That observation prompted the formation of an advisory committee and the publication in 1985 of an analysis of cultural and social structural barriers to health care, *Sociocultural Barriers to Appropriate Health Care for Ethnic Minorities*. In 1987, the department created a 30-member multi-ethnic coalition, three men and three women from five different minority groups, to advise the department and create goals and strategies. The two primary objectives were to collect data (because information about minority health needs was so limited), and to ensure that people of varied ethnic backgrounds are included in decision-making groups.

Two additional initiatives exist. One is an ongoing arrangement with the state Office of Primary Care and Rural Health, funded by the federal Health Care Financing Administration, to continue to translate information into multiple languages (including Navajo, if practical) and culturally relevant formats. The second is a plan to produce a cross-cultural awareness manual for all health care providers and perhaps for all state employees. Three of the five sections have been drafted. The Native American section will have five subparts, one for each tribe (Goshute, Navajo, Paiute, Shoshone, and Ute), to reflect the variation in attitudes toward health care among tribes.

Wisconsin. In 1993, the Wisconsin Legislature created the State Council on Indian Health to develop an American Indian Health Plan for improvement of health care services to Indian people. The plan is to address availability of health services, access, intergovernmental coordination, training of health care providers, and health care research. A grant program to support cooperative Indian health projects was also authorized.

Education

State-tribal cooperation in education can serve as a model for a new state-tribal-federal partnership in Native American education. Several states have implemented legislation to address shortcomings in an educational system that historically has disregarded the culture and heritage of American Indians and their contributions to the United States. Yet a great many educational issues still must be dealt with if high school completion rates and higher education retention rates are to improve significantly for Native American students.

Most of the nation's 400,000 Indian students attend public schools, many in inner city areas. Approximately 3 percent attend private schools. About 10 percent attend schools operated or funded by the Bureau of Indian Affairs (BIA). Tribal governments contract with the BIA to operate 73 of those schools.

Studies indicate that a third of Indian students who enter high school drop out. At the urging of Indian communities and tribal education leaders, some states have taken significant steps to review the educational needs of Native Americans and pass laws that affect how Indian students and their public school peers are instructed about Native Americans. The following case studies describe their efforts.

Minnesota. The Minnesota American Indian Education Act of 1988 encourages districts and schools to provide elementary and secondary language and cultural education programs that, among other things, include instruction in American Indian language, literature, history, and culture. It provides for cooperative arrangements with alternative schools that integrate American Indian culture into their curricula. The act also allows districts to seek exemptions from teacher licensing requirements if compliance would make it difficult to hire qualified teachers of American Indian language and cultural education.

For example, the Legislature has approved control by the White Earth Reservation Tribal Council of the K-8 Pine Point public school. The tribal council has the same powers and duties as a school board. The school, which is subject to the same instruction standards as other public schools, is eligible to receive federal aids and grants, as well as the same aid, revenues, and grants that local school districts receive. The Minnesota Legislature also appropriated more than $4 million in 1993 for Indian scholarships and grants.

**Rosebud Sioux Tribe
Education Code**

The Rosebud Sioux Tribe's agreement with South Dakota implements a Tribal Education Code under which the schools on the Rosebud Sioux reservation will teach tribal traditions, culture, history, and language.

According to Melody McCoy, senior staff attorney with the Native American Rights Fund: "Indian education at Rosebud today mirrors the national picture. The population of the reservation in 1990 was about 8,300, 2,500 of whom are school-age children. About 85 percent of the children go to public elementary and secondary schools operated by Todd County School District. The other 15 percent go to the St. Francis Indian School, a school operated through a charter by the tribe."

The Tribal Education Code was developed by representatives of the Native American Rights Fund who in turn represented the Tribal Council's Education Committee and the state of South Dakota, with the support of the Northwest Area Foundation and the Bush Foundation. The code recognizes the tribe's right to control education on its reservation, even when that education is provided by governments other than the tribe. According to McCoy, the goal behind the code's October 1991 adoption by the Tribal Council is multifaceted so ". . . the tribe could marshal and coordinate all the reservation education resources with the goals of reclaiming its youth, perpetuating the tribe and improving the systems."

Source: *Native American Legal Review*, Winter 1992.

Montana. American Indians are Montana's largest minority group, representing approximately 6 percent of the state's population. Native Americans reside on seven reservations and in communities within the state's major urban areas. When the Montana constitution was rewritten in 1972, the framers noted, "The state recognizes the distinct and unique cultural heritage of the American Indians and is committed in its educational goals to the preservation of their cultural integrity." According to the legislative Committee on Indian Affairs, the state has adopted a number of policies designed to implement this commitment.

In 1988, the state began the Minorities in Montana Education Project to enhance minority educational achievement. In 1989, the commissioner of higher education, with the assistance of a Ford Foundation grant, began the Tracks Project to address the high dropout rate of Indian students from public schools. One outcome of the Tracks Project was creation of the Office of Minority Achievement in the Office of the Commissioner of Higher Education. A one-year grant from the State Higher Education Executive Officers, continued with support from the Northwest Area Foundation, led to a 1991 two-year appropriation of $175,000 from the Montana Legislature. The funds supported the position of director of American Indian and Minority Education within the Office of the Commissioner of Higher Education. The director is responsible for collecting and analyzing data in conjunction with the Office of Public Instruction, making recommendations to the board of regents, acting as liaison between the state and the tribal colleges, and acting as a consultant to the university college system for recruitment and retention of minority students. The Office of Public Instruction will use this information to help schools develop goals and activities to meet the needs of Native American students. School districts with significant Indian enrollment may require certified personnel to take instruction in American Indian studies. The Montana University System offers a fee waiver to Indian students to assist them in attending a school in the system. The governor recently appointed an Indian to the Board of Regents for the first time in that board's history.

Oklahoma. The Oklahoma State Board of Education released *Native Americans: Leaders in the 21st Century* in December 1992. The report represents a joint effort among the 36 tribes in the state and the state Department of Education to cut Indian dropout rates in public schools and to make all students aware of Indian contributions to American culture. Saying that Oklahoma's 80,000 students "desperately need more Indian teachers, more Indian language instruction, and more sensitivity from educators," the report suggests that foreign language requirements could be met by American Indian language instruction, which would expand public school curriculums to include language and cultural aspects of the Indian experience in Oklahoma and the United States.

Wisconsin. The Wisconsin Department of Public Instruction began offering units on Indian history and tribal government in 1986. The Legislature has since enacted legislation requiring Indian education as a component of multicultural education.

Wisconsin Act 31 (1989) contains two provisions relating to American Indian curriculum. First, the state superintendent of public instruction is required, in coordination with the American Indian Language and Culture Education Board, to develop a curriculum for grades four through 12 concerning the Chippewa Indians' treaty-based, off-reservation rights to hunt, fish, and gather. The Wisconsin Department of Public Instruction has published *Classroom Activities on Chippewa Treaty Rights*. Second, each school board is required, as part of the social studies curriculum, to include instruction in the history, culture, and tribal sovereignty of the federally recognized American Indian tribes and bands in Wisconsin. Instruction must take place at least twice in the elementary grades and at least once in high school.

Act 31 also requires that each school board provide a program designed to give pupils at all grade levels an understanding of human relations, particularly with regard to American Indians, black Americans, and Hispanics. In addition, Act 31 requires that a teaching license not be granted unless the person has received instruction in minority group relations, including the history, culture, and tribal sovereignty of the federally recognized American Indian tribes and bands in Wisconsin.

Schools with a native focus. Most American Indian youth attend public schools and usually are either considered minorities or are not identified as members of any unique group. But about 15 percent, or 6,000 youngsters, are students at either private schools or Indian-run schools. These schools have been established explicitly to educate Native American children. They include mission schools, Bureau of Indian Affairs schools, and tribal schools.

Mission schools. Mission schools began during the late 19th century (with some exceptions going back to the 16th century in California and the Southwest) as a response to the practice of the federal government of taking land and giving it to various religious organizations. Episcopalians, Methodists, Lutherans, and Quakers were among the religious groups that established schools for Native Americans.

The Bureau of Catholic Indian Missions (BCIM) began in 1874 to educate Native American children. Today the BCIM supports many priests, sisters, lay workers, and teachers on reservations and in urban centers of the United States. In 1992, the BCIM gave more than $3 million for Native American education. Catholic mission schools include St. Labre in Ashland, Mont., Red Cloud Indian High School on the Pine Ridge Reservation in South Dakota, and St. Joseph in Chamberlain, S.D.

Bureau of Indian Affairs (BIA) schools. The federal BIA funds or operates 180 schools with 40,000 students in 26 states, representing about 10 percent of the nation's Native American student population. In 1991, the U.S. Department of the Interior conducted an investigation of 153 BIA schools, finding that only two were performing at the national median. Student performance was well below grade level, with average standardized test scores falling near the 25th percentile. Schools exhibited a lack of academic standards, inequitable financing, and unsafe school buildings.

An audit prepared by the Interior Department's inspector general concluded that, "Native American students at BIA schools have not received a quality education. These conditions occurred because senior-level bureau managers have generally not given the education program sufficient priority." The BIA's Office of Indian Education Programs has had 17 directors in the past 12 years. This information suggests that the federal role in educating Native American children should be revisited.

Tribal colleges. In 1990, 103,000 Indian people were enrolled in college. Currently in the United States, there are 29 tribally-controlled colleges and colleges operated by BIA, with 13,000 full and part-time students. Fifteen of the tribal colleges are accredited, and another eight are under consideration. Almost all the Indian colleges are two-year community colleges offering associate degrees in vocational or general education programs. Three exceptions are the four-year Oglala Lakota and Sinte Gleska colleges in South Dakota and Salish Kootenai College in Montana. Montana is the only state with a tribal college located on each reservation.

Tribal colleges are not funded by the states in which they operate except in Nebraska and Minnesota. Congress did authorize $5,820 for each student in 1978, yet less than half of that sum has been appropriated in recent years. Indian colleges receive no government funding for non-Indian students, who make up more than 15 percent of their student population.

Indian Nations at Risk

A 1991 report entitled *Indian Nations At Risk* concluded that all school systems' resources and programs must align to meet the needs of Native Americans rather than depend on special grant programs and Native-operated alternative schools. The report recommended new steps to halt the erosion of Indian cultures, including more funding for early childhood education and the infusion of Indian culture and heritage into public school curricula. The 15-member Indian Nations at Risk task force agreed on the adoption of Native Education Goals based generally on the National Education Goals endorsed in 1989 by President Bush and the nation's governors. The task force also adopted an Indian Student Bill of Rights enumerating the opportunities to which every American Indian and Alaska Native student is entitled:

- A safe and psychologically comfortable environment in school.

- A linguistic and cultural environment in school that offers students opportunities to maintain and develop a firm knowledge base.

- An intellectually challenging program in school that meets community needs as well as individual academic needs.

- A stimulating early childhood educational environment that is linguistically, culturally, and developmentally appropriate.

- Equity in school programs, facilities, and finances across Native communities and in schools run by the federal government and public schools in general.

Though not well known, these institutions play a significant role in Native American higher education. Tribal colleges "have reversed an appalling statistic," U.S. Senator Ben Nighthorse Campbell says. "Nine out of 10 Indian students who go directly from high school to a mainstream college fail. Nine out of 10 who go to a tribal college succeed; they get jobs, or continue their education. They turn out educated and capable citizens who contribute to their families, their tribes and their country."

Child Welfare

The federal Indian Child Welfare Act of 1978 (ICWA) (P.L. 95-608) is a law that protects the rights of Indian children, families, and tribes. It requires states and tribes to craft agreements to promote the welfare of Indian children. All provisions of the act are in effect if just one of the child's biological parents is Indian.

In 1968, the Association on American Indian Affairs conducted a survey on Indian child custody proceedings that served to initiate a 10-year process of hearings and reports. This activity demonstrated to Congress that state courts and welfare departments were removing an inordinately high proportion (25 percent-35 percent) of Indian children from their homes and tribes and placing them in non-Indian homes and institutions. Non-Indian couples adopted 90 percent of the tribal children.

When Does ICWA Apply?

The Indian Child Welfare Act of 1978 protects the Indian child who is:

- Determined by a federally recognized tribe to be a member or eligible for membership,

- Under 18 years of age,

- Unmarried,

- The biological child of a member of an Indian tribe.

The act does not apply in juvenile cases resulting from a child's delinquent actions or in child custody cases or divorce proceedings.

As a result, concern arose that many Indian children were losing their cultural identity and tribes were losing their greatest resource—the next generation of tribal members. Congress concluded that "the Indian child welfare crisis is of massive proportions and that Indian families face vastly greater risks of involuntary separation than are typical of our society as a whole." The crisis was caused by a failure of "states, exercising their recognized jurisdiction over Indian child custody proceedings through administrative and judicial bodies . . . to recognize the essential tribal relations of Indian people and the cultural and social standards prevailing in Indian communities and families."

The result was enactment of the ICWA. The ICWA provides for establishment of minimum federal standards for the removal of Indian children from their families; for the placement of Indian children in homes that reflect the unique values of Indian culture; and for assistance to Indian tribes in the operation of child and family service programs. Such programs strive to ensure that an Indian child is permanently removed from parental custody only as a last resort.

Minimum federal standards of evidence established under the act must be met before an Indian child may be removed from his or her family temporarily. In addition, an expert witness knowledgeable in Indian customs and social relations must testify. The decision to place a child in foster care must be based solely on a family's ability to provide a suitable home by the standards of their Indian community. These provisions protect Indian families from potentially culturally biased judgments of non-Indian court systems. Courts can, however, temporarily bypass these provisions in emergencies when a child is in immediate physical danger. In such emergency placements, the agency must expeditiously initiate a child custody proceeding under the provisions of the ICWA. The child's parent or tribe may request transfer of the child to the tribe's jurisdiction and this transfer must be granted, unless the state can show good cause to the contrary.

In all involuntary removal proceedings involving an Indian child (or a child that the court has reason to believe is Indian), the state court must notify the child's parents or Indian custodian and the child's tribe of their right to intervene in the case. If the child's tribal affiliation is not known, the court must notify the regional office of the BIA. The bureau, upon receipt of state court notification, has 15 days to notify the child's parents or Indian custodian and the child's tribe. Upon the receipt of written notification, the tribe has 10 days to respond, although an additional 20 days may be granted if requested.

Often, however, such a system is not applicable to Native Americans living in urban areas, and often cases are not reported to the child's tribe, or the tribe cannot afford to bring the child back to the reservation for the hearing. In these cases, jurisdiction is turned over to the state court systems.

In all foster care, preadoptive, and adoptive placements, preference is given, unless there is good cause to the contrary, to placing the child with one of the following:

- A member of the child's extended family,
- Other members of the child's tribe,
- An Indian foster home or adoptive family,
- An Indian-operated institution,
- A non-Indian family or institution, if there is no other choice.

When the tribe chooses to intervene in a case, the state court must give "full faith and credit" to the judicial proceedings of the tribal court. In some instances, the tribe may choose to have a "transfer of jurisdiction," in which case the legal proceedings are transferred to the tribal court, unless the state can show good cause why it should not be transferred.

Indian child welfare agreements between states and tribes. Section 109(a) of the federal Indian Child Welfare Act provides that states and Indian tribes are authorized to enter into agreements with each other with respect to the care and custody of Indian children and jurisdiction over child custody proceedings, including agreements that may provide for orderly transfer of jurisdiction case by case and agreements that provide for concurrent jurisdiction of states and Indian tribes. Numerous agreements are in place.

New Mexico. New Mexico and the Navajo Nation signed a 1985 agreement under the state's Joint Powers Agreement Act of 1978 that was "predicated on a government-to-government relationship between the State of New Mexico and the Navajo Nation in a spirit of cooperation, coordination, communication, and good will." The state and the tribe agreed that the agreement's primary purpose was to protect and further the best interests of Navajo children; therefore, the agreement "seeks to promote and strengthen the unity and security between the Navajo child and his or her natural family. The primary considerations in the placement of a Navajo child are to insure that the child is raised within the Navajo culture, that the child is raised within his or her family where possible and that the child is raised as an Indian."

Montana. All seven of the reservations in Montana have signed agreements with the state on Indian child welfare. One agreement is called Tribal Foster Care Services (4-E), whereby the state agreed that the tribe will license its own foster homes to which the state will make payment. The tribe also contracted for a state-paid social worker and a secretary located on the reservation to provide foster care services.

South Dakota. The South Dakota Department of Child Protective Services has the most comprehensive data on child abuse among American Indians of the states that responded to a survey conducted by the American Indian Health Care Association. Many states are able to give totals for types of abuse and age categories, but are not able to break down the data by race. South Dakota publishes an annual statistical report that covers child abuse and neglect investigation and placement. The report includes tables of substantiated numbers by age and sex on American Indians and Alaska Natives. Such thorough state statistics on child abuse and neglect, though rare, are extremely helpful both to tribal governments and to state agencies.

This chapter has discussed how states and tribes are working together in the policy areas of health, education, and child welfare. Sluggish economies in many areas of Indian country contribute to poverty and limited futures for many Indian people. The next chapter discusses some of the state-tribal efforts designed to foster healthier economic conditions.

References

American Indian Health Care Association. *Assessment of the Health Needs of American Indians/Alaska Natives Living in Cities Not Served by an Urban Indian Health Program Funded by Indian Health Service.* Minneapolis: AIHCA, September 1992.

American Indian Health Care Association. *Report on the Status of the Indian Child Welfare Act of 1978 Among Urban American Indians and Alaska Natives.* St. Paul, Minn.: AIHCA, November 1992.

Association of State and Territorial Health Organizations. *Bilingual Health Initiative Report and Recommendations: State Health Agency Strategies to Develop Linguistically Relevant Public Health Systems.* Washington, D.C.: ASTHO, July 1992.

California Department of Health Services, Health Promotion Section. *American Indian Task Force Report on the Year 2000 Health Promotion Objectives and Recommendations for California.* Sacramento: California DHS, 1992.

Denver Indian Health and Family Services. *Indian Child Welfare Program* (brochure), Denver, Colo., no date.

Hooker, Tracey, and Lucinda Bryant. *HIV/AIDS Fact to Consider: August 1992 Update.* Denver: National Conference of State Legislatures, 1992.

Indian Child Welfare Act, 25 U.S.C. Sec. 1901 et seq.

"Indian Child Welfare Act Agreement Between the New Mexico Human Services Department and the Navajo Tribe." September 17, 1985.

Indian Health Service. *Comprehensive Health Care Program for American Indians and Alaska Natives.* Washington. D.C.: U.S. Department of Health and Human Services, Public Health Service, n.d.

Indian Health Service. *Trends in Indian Health 1991.* Washington, D.C.: U.S. Department of Health and Human Services, Public Health Service, 1991.

Larson, Lisa. "Education Laws Affecting Indian Students." In *Indians, Indian Tribes and State Government.* St. Paul: Research Department, Minnesota House of Representatives, February 1993.

Michigan Law Revision Commission. "Study Report: Michigan's Legislative Power Over Its Native American Population." In *28th Annual Report 1993.* Ann Arbor, Mich.: West Publishing Co., 1993.

Montana Committee on Indian Affairs. *The Tribal Nations of Montana: A Handbook for Legislators.* Helena, Mont.: Montana Legislative Council, March 1995.

South Dakota Legislative Research Council. *Nursing Home and Alternative Services Provided to Elderly Native Americans.* Issue Memorandum 95-03, written by Jeff Bostic, May 18, 1995.

Stiffarm, Jonny BearCub. "History, Guidelines, and Highlights of the Act." In *Indian Child Welfare Act: A Pro Bono Training.* Denver: Council of Energy Resource Tribes, March 1992.

"Topics in Minority Health: Alcohol-Related Hospitalizations--Indian Health Service and Tribal Hospitals, United States, May 1992." *Morbidity and Mortality Weekly Report.* 41, no. 41, (October 16, 1992).

U.S. Department of Education. *Indian Nations At Risk: An Educational Strategy for Action,* October 1991. Final report of the Indian Nations at Risk Task Force.

U.S. Secretary of Health and Human Services (with the assistance of the Indian Health Service, American Indian and Alaska Native People). *Annual Report to Congress on Tribal Contract Costs Associated with Indian Self-Determination Contracts: the Indian Self-Determination and Education Act Amendments of 1933, Public Law 100-472.* March 1992.

Wisconsin, 1993 Assembly Bill 296, "An Act...Creating A Council on American Indian Health, preparation of an American Indian health plan and cooperative American Indian health projects..."

Zelio, Judy, and Tracey Hooker, ed. *Protecting Our Young People's Future: HIV Prevention for Native Americans--A Roundtable for State Legislators, Tribal Leaders and State Health Officials.* Denver: National Conference of State Legislatures, May 1994.

Note: The legislative history for the Indian Child Welfare Act primarily appears in two documents: H.R. Rep. No. 1386, 95th Cong., 2nd Sess.; and Part III, Department of the Interior, Bureau of Indian Affairs; Guidelines for State Courts; Indian Child Custody Proceedings, 44 Fed. Reg. 67,584 (November 26, 1979).

5. STATE-TRIBAL ECONOMIC DEVELOPMENT PARTNERSHIPS

Partnerships between states and Indian tribes to promote economic development are a new but growing phenomenon. By working cooperatively, each participating entity can realize benefits not available outside of the partnership. Tribal governments are increasing economic opportunities for tribal members through partnerships with business and industry, through federal programs, and through nurturing home-grown businesses and micro-enterprises. State-tribal agreements create another way to enhance economic progress on tribal land and in adjacent rural areas. Several examples of state-tribal accords are profiled in this chapter.

The economic condition of Native Americans today is the result of centuries of cultural and economic domination by non-Indians combined with the legacy of federal paternalism. Although the BIA now espouses a policy of self-determination and tribal control over tribal affairs, it monitors tribal economic development closely, exerting federal control over financial relationships and economic ties on the reservations. Earlier federal policies ranging from trade restrictions between Indians and non-Indians in the early 1800s to formal assimilation and relocation policies through the 1950s have created real and perceived obstacles to economic development on tribal lands that tribal governments are working to overcome.

Viable Partnerships

Indian tribal governments are improving their economic situation by taking control of their own environmental, financial, and human resources for the benefit of the tribe and by entering partnerships where beneficial. Tribal economic development approaches are as numerous and diverse as the tribes themselves.

Yet tensions exist within Indian tribes over whether to seek economic development opportunities that may threaten environmental, cultural, and religious traditions. Each tribe sorts these questions out for itself, but increasingly the choice embraces some form of economic endeavor so the tribe can survive and flourish into the next century.

The Lakota Fund. Large American financial institutions have hesitated to lend to tribes, but Native Americans are finding other, innovative means to fund economic development. The Lakota Fund, started in 1987, is an enterprising loan fund operating successfully on the Pine Ridge Indian reservation located in the poorest county in the United States. The Lakota Fund survived a shaky start and now operates the Circle Banking Project for micro-enterprise lending. Members of the Oglala Sioux Tribe can form circles of four to six people who are willing to act as co-debtors to each other's loans. Each individual in the circle is granted a loan to become involved in a separate micro-enterprise.

The circles help household-based enterprises become viable businesses. The loan program includes business finance workshops to educate the circle members on loan terms and basic finance. The Lakota Fund has found that the Circle Banking Project has a much higher repayment rate than individual loans, perhaps because of the peer pressure of the lending circle and the personal responsibility each feels to the circle members. The fund's success has attracted additional capital from banks and foundations. Developments in computer telecommunications and information technology are likely to promote a new kind of tribal micro-enterprise.

Indian business loan program. An Indian business loan program has operated in Minnesota since it was enacted by the Legislature in 1973. This program provides Indians in Minnesota with opportunities to establish new businesses or to improve existing enterprises and provides management resources and business technical assistance for clients. The loan program is funded through mineral rights taxes collected annually by counties and allocated among the 11 reservations in Minnesota. Loans are administered by the state, but individual tribal councils determine which projects receive funding.

The Menominee Tribe in Wisconsin operates a $1 million revolving loan program out of gaming revenues to assist individuals in business startups or expansions.

Tribal Government Assistance Program. Housed within the Small Business Division of the Oklahoma Department of Commerce, the Tribal Government Assistance Program provides support and technical assistance for economic development projects on American Indian trust lands. The office assists with preparing and analyzing business plans, locating capital sources, coordinating meetings between lender and borrower, and devising investment procedures that comply with federal-Indian trust status. In addition to offering economic technical assistance, the Tribal Government Assistance Program established an Indian advisory council that meets at least four times per year and has held annual Indian economic development conferences for tribal governments.

Other enterprises. Areas under tribal jurisdiction can qualify as "enterprise zones" under legislation passed by Nebraska in 1993 (L.B. 725). The Enterprise Zone Act gives tax credits to businesses that locate in enterprise zones. Enterprise zones are defined as economically distressed areas. Wisconsin's Development Zone Program requires that two of 15 authorized zones include all or a portion of an Indian reservation.

The Passamaquoddy Tribe Enters the Pollution Control Market

After subsisting on farming and fishing for centuries, the Passamaquoddy tribe won $40 million in a land claim suit against the state of Maine in 1980. The tribe sought investment advice, then purchased New England's only cement plant. The tribe propelled the flagging company into a successful enterprise. Along the way, the Passamaquoddies hired a geochemist to solve the plant's dust emissions problem. The resulting technology not only will cut dust emissions from cement factories, it may change the way America burns coal.

The "Recovery Scrubber" uses waste ash and acid emissions and recycles them, cutting emissions from the plant by over 90 percent. The recycled products (fertilizer, limestone, and distilled water) are non-hazardous, useful commodities. Other scrubbers exist, but they introduce new and expensive chemicals to the scrubbing process and produce a solid waste which must be taken to a landfill. The Recovery Scrubber not only recycles kiln dust, but it cuts sulfur dioxide and carbon dioxide emissions.

The cement industry in the U.S. and abroad will soon be installing the scrubber and plans are underway to modify the scrubber for use on coal-fired power stations. In fact, Tom Tureen, chairman of the scrubber marketing firm Passamaquoddy Technology, states that the scrubber could cut by as much as one-third the 10 million tons of sulfur dioxide that must be reduced annually to comply with the Clean Air Act Amendments of 1990. Even companies that have already met those requirements could install the Recovery Scrubber to sell the "rights" to their increased emission reductions under Clean Air Act rules.

The tribe sold the company in 1983, but patented the scrubber and are currently marketing the pollution control device around the world. The Passamaquoddies also own one of the largest wild blueberry farms in the world and market their own blueberry ice cream. The financial acumen of the Passamaquoddy tribe is used as a case study by Harvard Business School.

The Colorado Department of Transportation worked with the Ute Mountain Ute tribe to develop a transit plan to meet the needs of tribal residents. If fully implemented, the plan will assist tribal members in their access to jobs, education, and health care through an integrated program of lending official tribal vehicles to a tribal transit system.

The Oklahoma Legislature passed the Government-to-Government Act (S.B. 210) in 1988, which authorized the state to enter into intergovernmental compacts with federally recognized tribes to discuss issues of mutual concern. This law opened the door to economic development assistance and opportunities on reservations.

Tribes also are undertaking innovations that include direct-mail fund raising. The Anishinaabe people of White Earth, Minn., are buying back portions of their traditional land base through private contributions, with matching funds from the White Earth Tribal government. The stated goal is to build a base for economic growth and cultural survival.

A 1989 Wisconsin legislative study of economic development on Indian reservations identified barriers to participation by tribes in the state's economic development programs, with instructions to the Department of Development to eliminate them. Several statutes were discovered to be impediments because they were drafted with no recognition of tribes, their status, and needs. Oregon allows tribes to access state economic development programs in the same manner as communities and businesses.

A few tribes and states also are working together to promote Native American art, culture, and historic places to increase tourism. South Dakota launched a tourism marketing plan in 1991 that relied heavily on the Native American cultural influence in the state. A principal objective of the marketing plan was to "increase Native American annual tourism receipts by 100 percent within five years." Several states, including Arizona, Montana, New Mexico, Oklahoma, and South Dakota, have enacted legislation to protect Native American arts and crafts from nonauthentic copies.

Some tribes have found other revenue-producing uses for their land. Tribes have opened resort hotels and meeting facilities on their lands. The White Mountain Apache tribe in east-central Arizona has attracted visitors with a seven-lift ski resort on their land, which brings in $9 million per year in revenue. In New Mexico, Ski Apache, owned by the Mescalero Apache Tribe, also brings significant tourist revenue to the tribe and the nearby non-Indian town of Ruidoso. The tribe also operates a four-star resort called Inn of the Mountain Gods.

Natural Resources

A number of tribes, particularly in the West, are using their natural resources to sustain the tribe economically and to diversify into other enterprises. Indian reservations contain a wealth of minerals, including 5 percent of the U.S. oil and gas reserves, 30 percent of the strippable low-sulfur coal, and 50 percent to 60 percent of the uranium. In 1990 more than 15 million barrels of oil, 135 million cubic feet of natural gas, and 27 million tons of coal were produced from American Indian lands. Even if tribes do not mine these minerals themselves, they may lease those rights to others. They have the right, upheld by the Supreme Court in 1982, to tax non-Indian mineral development on reservation land. The Uintah and Ouray Ute Indian Tribe of Utah has generated substantial income from leasing mineral rights on its land, as have other tribes in Arizona, Colorado, Montana, and New Mexico.

Real Indicators of Tribal Economies

The key economic indicators for tribal economies are (1) the gross reservation product (comparable to gross domestic product), (2) economic leakage, and (3) the economic multiplier.

First, the gross reservation product, the wealth produced by reservation economies, does not explain Indian poverty. For most tribes, sufficient wealth is produced to support a much higher standard of living.

Second, economic leakage [wealth leaving the reservation economy] is nearly 90 percent. Though individual Indian consumption of goods and services bought from off-reservation business is the visible form of this leakage, it actually represents a very small percentage (about 10 percent) of the leakage. The major leakages are debt service to non-Indian lenders, including the federal government; non-Indian leases of Indian lands and natural resources; payments to non-Indian utilities; and state taxes on non-Indian working interests in minerals and mining.

Third, the economic multiplier is depressed. This indicator measures the degree to which a dollar of income stimulates additional economic activity. The multiplier for tribal economies ranges from .9 to 1.19, while border town economies average 2.28. This means that for tribes a dollar of income to the economy generates 90 cents to $1.19 compared with $2.28 for the border town. In comparison, the national multiplier is about 3.0.

Federal Indian programs of more ancient vintage—Bureau of Indian Affairs (BIA), Indian Health Service (IHS) and, to a lesser but still sizable degree, Housing and Urban Development—contribute to the high leakage and low multiplier, thus counter-productively contributing to poor performance of tribal economies. A hidden but important part of the federal drag on tribal economies is the low value assigned to Indian lands and resources in the past by BIA. In the early years, rights-of-way and mineral leases were negotiated by the Interior Department at values far below true economic value. These economic savings flow to non-Indian state economies in the form of lower prices and increased profits, depriving the tribal economies of their benefits. Although current practices have ended these historic inequities for current agreements, nearly all Indian mineral leases and rights-of-way are still operated under terms patently unfair to the Indian landowners. The difference in values is best illustrated by comparing BIA values assigned to rights-of-way with what tribes actually receive when they negotiate on their own using through-put and value-added valuation methodologies. These new methods result in payments of 75 to 150 times the value assigned by the Department of Interior.

BIA and IHS services that consume more than three-fourths of the $4 billion in federal Indian expenditures have an 88 percent leakage before the dollar reaches the tribal economy in the form of a service. By the government "doing for" the tribe rather than assisting the tribe to do work itself, there is little to no technology transfer from the government to the tribe and its work force. Also, the education and training provided is focused on preparing Indians to work in the non-Indian, off-reservation economy rather than developing the tribal human resource to serve the future growth of the tribal economy.

More recently enacted federal assistance programs such as Head Start, the Native American Programs Act (ANA), the Self-Determination/Self-Governance Act, and others that directly fund the tribes promote not only local control, but local economic performance as well. The tribes hire local workers and use local materials, merchants, and suppliers with funds that benefit the local economy. But more important, these programs transfer technology and know-how to the tribe.

If the economic leakage were stanched and the multiplier were increased to the level of the reservation border towns, nearly 120,000 jobs would result. Finally, an interesting corollary to the indicators of tribal economies is that those tribes that are assertive of their sovereignty in enforcing land base control, negotiating their own resource agreements, and enforcing tribal employment and contracting rights are the tribes with the better performing economies and more favorable economic indicators. Thus, tribal politics is an important tool in improving tribal economies, contrary to popular notions.

—A. David Lester, Council of Energy Resource Tribes

Timber is a major asset of tribes in the North and Northwest. The Colville Indian Reservation in northern Washington was hit hard by the falling price of timber, although timber prices recently have risen because more old growth forests are being placed off limits to protect the spotted owl. For many tribes in the northern and northwestern United States, the timber industry was once the main provider of jobs on the reservation. In 1984, the tribal economic council organized the Colville Tribal Enterprise Corporation (CTEC) to exercise the commercial and business responsibilities of the tribe. CTEC developed the Colville Indian Precision Pine Company, which is the main tribal employer today.

Fishing rights are another means through which a few tribes obtain economic capital in addition to subsistence. The Swinomish Indian Tribe, located just north of Seattle, Wash., operates a large salmon fishery that is an important part of the economic and cultural well-being of the tribe, which has always subsisted on fish and marine life from the rich coastline and surrounding tributaries.

Natural resource development and land use often have been points of contention for states and tribes. States fear that tribal governments will not require environmental protection as stringent as state and federal standards for mining operations or waste sites. Tribes also fear environmental degradation. With adequate environmental safeguards, and state-tribal cooperation in developing those safeguards, natural resource development on reservation lands has many beneficial implications for the state's economy.

Taxation and Gaming

The issues of reservation-based taxation and gaming are addressed in more detail in chapters 6 and 7. Both are important aspects of Native American economic development and should be viewed as components of the larger picture of tribal prosperity.

Economic Partnerships Offer Links

Economic disputes create some of the most contentious issues for states and Indian tribes. Yet tribes are linked to states in environmental and economic affairs, and common solutions on relevant issues can be mutually beneficial.

States with Indian reservations have an often-untapped asset within their borders. Tribes have many mechanisms in place to attract business, increase tourism, and boost revenues in the state. The federal government and several states have provided an incentive structure to increase business enterprises to Indian reservations, including job training wage supplements for workers, direct loans, loan guarantees, grants and technical assistance, accelerated depreciation, and employment tax credits.

A recent study by the Center for Applied Research on the economic importance of tribes in Arizona concluded that "tribal governments obtain virtually all of their goods and services from vendors off the reservation, and this, in turn, supports jobs and sales and income tax payments to the state." The study found that Indian tribes are viable economic entities that contribute to the overall state economy: approximately $208 million is spent annually for goods and services off the reservation in Arizona.

States should be aware of the economic development opportunities available by bringing tourism to reservations. Native American art is admired all over the world, and people are increasingly interested in Indian culture and religion. States and tribes can work together to market the interesting and educational attractions in "Indian Country" and provide better access to some smaller, remote tribes that are not situated near a main highway. Bringing in tourists not only will provide jobs for tribal members, it will increase visits to existing non-Indian attractions.

Some American Indian tribes have been reluctant to embrace free-market capitalism and competitive individualism because of conflict with Native American culture, religion, and daily life. However, many tribes have found that economically stable projects that benefit the entire tribe need not invariably conflict with traditional values. To the extent that tribes are willing, states have much to gain by assisting Indian tribes to become economically viable entities in their state. A decline in unemployment and the corresponding decrease in state assistance is one benefit that states will enjoy. In addition, states will benefit indirectly from an increase in industry, tax base, and service sector jobs. The effects on tribal lands of the recent development of the gambling casino industry are only beginning to become available for study. The next chapter examines the statutory foundations for that industry.

References

Anding, Thomas L., and Evan R. Fulton. "Transportation on Remote Indian Reservations." *Center for Urban and Regional Affairs Reporter* (University of Minnesota) 23, no. 4 (December 1993): 1-6.

American Indian Resources Institute. *Indian Tribes as Sovereign Governments: A Sourcebook on Federal-Tribal History, Law and Policy.* Oakland, Calif.: AIRI Press, 1988.

Center for Applied Research. *The Economic and Fiscal Importance of Indian Tribes in Arizona.* Denver, Center for Applied Research, 1993.

"Clean Emissions, Valuable By-Products." *International Cement Review* (March 1991).

Commission on State Tribal Relations, *Handbook on State-Tribal Relations.* Albuquerque, N.M.: American Indian Law Center; and Denver: National Conference of State Legislatures, 1983.

Cornell, Stephen, and Joseph Kalt. "Pathways for Poverty: Economic Development and Institution-Building on American Indian Reservations." *American Indian Culture and Research Journal* 14, no. 1 (1990): 89-125.

Hamilton, Candy. "The Lakota Fund." *Winds of Change* (American Indian Engineering Society) (Autumn 1994): 64-71.

"Indians and Europe Are Doing Business in the 1980s and 1990s." *Denver Post,* April 7, 1990.

The Lakota Fund: A Program of First Nations Financial Project. Falmouth, Va.: First Nations Financial Project, February 1989.

McGlone, Deidre. "Building Economic Opportunity on Indian Reservations," *GW Policy Perspectives* (George Washington University) (Spring 1994).

Minnesota Indian Affairs Council. *Annual Report.* St. Paul, Minn.: November 15, 1988.

Morin, Kimberly A. *1994 State Legislation on Native American Issues.* Denver: National Conference of State Legislatures, September 1994.

Nebraska, LB 725, 1993.

Northwest Renewable Resources Center. *Indian Land Tenure and Economic Development Project: Phase I.* Seattle, Wash.: NRRC, 1987.

Oklahoma Department of Commerce. *Tribal Government Assistance Program. 1989 Annual Report.* Oklahoma City, Okla.: Small Business Division, Department of Commerce, 1990.

Reed, James B. "1991 State Legislation Relating to Native Americans." *NCSL State Legislative Report* 16, no. 9, December 1991.

Shonka, Molly. "Facilitating Economic Development: State & Tribal Partnerships." Washington, D.C.: National Governors' Association, January 1995.

Smith, Tim. "Financing Economic and Business Development on Indian Reservations: Fulfilling the Promise of Self-Determination." *Northwest Report* (1990): 20-34.

South Dakota Task Force on Tourism. "Partnership for Development." *A Travel Marketing Plan for South Dakota*. January 1991.

"State Policy and Economic Development in Oklahoma: 1989." *Report to Oklahoma 2000 Inc.* Oklahoma City, Okla.: January 1989.

"A Tribe of Innovators." *Financial Times*. April 26, 1991.

Ute Indian Tribe and the Uintah Basin Association of Government. *Uintah and Ouray Indian Reservation* (brochure). Fort Duchesne, Utah.

White-Tail Feather, Alex; James B. Reed; and Judy Zelio. *State-Tribal Legislation 1992 and 1993 Summaries*. Denver, Colo.: National Conference of State Legislatures, February 1994.

6. STATES AND THE INDIAN GAMING REGULATORY ACT

Indian tribes and states together face new legal, social, and economic challenges with the development of casino gambling and other high-stakes gaming on Indian lands.

A number of tribes, believing that gambling is a way to quickly achieve economic self-sufficiency, have established various high-stakes gaming activities that are considered illegal under the laws of the states in which their lands lie. Some states' officials have challenged the tribes' right to do so.

Indian tribal gaming thus has moved to the forefront of state-tribal relations, sparking debates over where, what kind, and how much gambling will take place. Economic development has been a prime concern for tribal governments for many years, but success has been elusive. Now it seems that tribes may have found a moneymaking activity to significantly improve living conditions for their members (and other nearby community members as well), at least in the short run. Their success has created a competitive environment that has helped spread high-stakes gambling across the country.

Indian Gaming Regulatory Act

In 1988, Congress passed the Indian Gaming Regulatory Act (IGRA). The act outlines a process by which states and tribes can reach agreement about the conduct of Indian gaming. IGRA attempts to recognize the existing state role in gaming regulation by dividing Indian gaming into three classes. Two classes of Indian gaming fall under Indian and federal control. The third, "Class III," or casino-style, gaming, is acknowledged to be a state-tribal issue.

IGRA describes Class I gaming as "social games played solely for prizes of minimal value or traditional forms of Indian gaming engaged in as a part of, or in connection with, tribal ceremonies or celebrations." Class I gaming is under the exclusive jurisdiction of Indian tribes and is not subject to any provision of IGRA.

IGRA defines Class II gaming as "the game of chance commonly known as bingo . . . including (if played in the same location) pull tabs, lotto, punch boards, tip jars, instant bingo, and other games similar to bingo." IGRA also includes bingo games conducted with "electronic, computer, or other technologic aids" as Class II gaming. But the act excludes "electronic or electromechanical facsimiles of any game of chance or slot machines of any kind" from Class II gaming.

Nonbanking card games are permissible under Class II gaming, unless they are explicitly prohibited by state law. "Banking card games" are described in the Senate committee report that accompanied the act as "those games where players play against the house and the house acts as banker" versus "nonbanking card games" where players play against each other.

Class II gaming is under extensive tribal jurisdiction but is subject to provisions of IGRA and oversight regulation by the National Indian Gaming Commission. Class II gaming is not subject to state regulation.

Tribes and states have expressed differing interpretations of IGRA's definition of Class II gaming. Court decisions have clarified some provisions, and the National Indian Gaming Commission has issued regulations clarifying several definitions.

The National Indian Gaming Commission, in regulations published on April 9, 1992, clarified several definitions. In particular, it specifically excluded the games known as "keno" and "bingojack" from Class II gaming. It reinforced the definition of lotto determined in the *Oneida* case. The commission also specified that games such as video bingo, in which a single player plays a game with or against a machine rather than with or against other players, are Class III gaming, not Class II.

IGRA designates Class III gaming as all other types of gambling, including banking card games (e.g., baccarat, chemin de fer, or blackjack), slot machines, pari-mutuel racing, and jai alai. Electronic games of chance, such as video poker, are also considered Class III gaming.

IGRA requires states and tribes to negotiate compacts establishing the rules by which Class III gaming on tribal lands will be conducted. Under IGRA, tribes may not legally conduct casino-style gambling without a "compact" that both state and tribe have agreed will provide the framework for the conduct of tribal gaming. The state-tribal gaming compact must be approved by the secretary of the interior before tribal gaming can proceed.

As of this writing, nearly 150 compacts have been approved in 24 states involving at least 123 tribes. Tribal gaming operations must be conducted on tribal land (reservation land or land held in trust for the tribe by the Interior Department). Although states may not tax the tribes' gambling revenues, compacts usually include provisions for a tribe to reimburse the state for costs of gambling regulation and administration. States that also have formal arrangements with tribes to receive additional funds from tribal gaming proceeds include Michigan, Connecticut, and Washington. Tribes in Massachusetts, New Mexico, and Rhode Island also propose to give some gaming revenues to the states.

Tribal casinos established under IGRA (with state-tribal negotiated compacts and with approval from the Interior Department) are located in Arizona, California, Colorado, Connecticut, Idaho, Iowa, Kansas, Louisiana, Michigan, Minnesota, Mississippi, Montana, Nebraska, Nevada, New Mexico, New York, North Carolina, North Dakota, Oregon, South Dakota, Washington, and Wisconsin. Compacts also have been signed in Oklahoma and Rhode Island. The financial success of tribal casinos varies greatly by location.

States and Indian Casino Gambling

IGRA creates difficult questions about who makes state public policy decisions. Thirty-four states now operate lotteries, and nine states allow some form of commercial casino gambling. Nontribal casinos in Colorado, Louisiana, Nevada, New Jersey, and South Dakota offer slots, roulettes, and card games to varying degrees as do riverboats in Illinois, Louisiana, Missouri, Iowa, and Mississippi. Many states permit charitable organizations to hold occasional "casino nights" as fund raisers.

Legislators across the country increasingly approve various forms of gambling with the expectation that the states will have a role in the regulation and oversight of gaming activities within state borders. But tribal high-stakes casino gambling allowed under IGRA, and so far supported by court decisions, is not subject to state control except as agreed to in compacts. Therefore, tribal gambling activities beyond the scope permitted to nontribal entities elsewhere in a state present a policy challenge to state lawmakers who consider high-stakes casino gambling to be contrary to the public interest. State law enforcement officials, concerned about crime, want a role in regulating tribal casino gaming. State revenue departments would like to tap into the flow of spending on gambling. Other officials wish to limit Indian gaming to avoid saturation of the limited gambling market. And state lawmakers want to ensure that the prevailing state gambling climate is what voters intended it to be. State efforts to have a hand in controlling tribal gaming have prompted cries of "economic racism" by some Indian people and raised issues of sovereignty.

Legislative reaction to the policymaking challenge has been slow, although lawmakers in a few states have begun to seek ways to stop further expansion of tribal casino gaming by enacting state legislation. They usually find themselves stymied, however, for at least two reasons. First, state laws do not apply on tribal lands. Second, because existing state laws do in fact allow various forms of gambling rather than prohibit it, tribes are permitted to proceed with similar forms of gambling.

By mid-1995, 14 states had statutes addressing state-tribal gaming compacts under IGRA. Eleven states specifically authorize governors to negotiate or enter into state-tribal gaming compacts; five states grant that authority to a commission or other state department or agency. The states that authorize governors to negotiate state-tribal gaming compacts include Arizona, Colorado, Idaho, Kansas, Louisiana, Minnesota, Nebraska, Oklahoma, South Dakota, Washington, and Wisconsin. The states that authorize state entities other than governors to negotiate state-tribal gaming compacts include California (Racing Board); Iowa (Department of Inspections and Appeals); Montana (public agencies negotiate state-tribal agreements of all types); South Dakota (Indian Affairs Commission); and Washington (Gambling Commission). Though the issue of a governor's authority to enter a compact with a tribe for gaming has been discussed in many states, it has been litigated in few. One decision on the topic was that of the Kansas Supreme Court in *Kansas ex rel. Stephan vs. Finney*, which held that the governor may enter into negotiations but without delegation of power from the legislature, may not bind the state to a compact. A July 1995 decision by the New Mexico Supreme Court held that the governor overstepped his executive powers by signing gaming compacts with 14 Indian pueblos and tribes without approval by the Legislature.

Legislative oversight of gambling compacts, once uncommon, is becoming more frequent. At least five states require legislative involvement in the approval of compacts. Idaho, Kansas, and Oklahoma authorize governors to negotiate compacts but also require legislative approval. Idaho law provides for legislative monitoring of all compact negotiations and requires legislative ratification of any compact that appropriates funds or authorizes forms of gaming otherwise prohibited by Idaho law. In Kansas, state-tribal compacts must be approved by the legislature, or if the legislature is not in session, the Legislative Coordinating Council. Kansas' legislation establishes the six-member Joint Committee on Gaming Compacts, which is authorized to develop guidelines to consider in reviewing compacts, hold public hearings on proposed compacts, and recommend changes to any proposed compacts. In Oklahoma, the Joint Committee on State-Tribal Relations oversees and approves all types of state-tribal agreements. Minnesota law requires the governor to include two members of the state Senate and two members of the House among the compact-negotiating designees, and those appointees must include the chairs of the house and senate committees with jurisdiction over gambling policy. Washington requires a standing committee from each chamber of the legislature to hold a public hearing on a compact and forward their comments to the gambling commission before the compact is executed by the governor.

Other provisions of state laws include requirements for public hearings concerning proposed gaming compacts and requirements that governors report periodically to the legislature on compact negotiations. In addition, several states designate specific departments, agencies, or officials to oversee Indian gaming (e.g., Arizona Department of Racing, Idaho state lottery director, Oklahoma State Bureau of Investigation). Louisiana authorizes the governor to appoint an Indian gaming commission to serve as the formal negotiating agent of the state.

Many of these state actions were taken in the early 1990s. It is obvious that, rather than wait for Congress to modify IGRA, state lawmakers have developed policies that reflect the concerns and needs of their constituents.

Issues in Negotiation

Limiting tribal gaming to the same gaming allowed under state law—the position adopted by many state negotiators and resisted by many tribal negotiators—could be accomplished in at least two ways: (1) by amending IGRA to require that tribal gaming conform to the same restrictions that apply elsewhere within a state's boundaries or (2) by gaining tribal agreement during the compact negotiation process to accept state limitations. Prohibiting certain forms of gaming entirely by enacting state legislation or amending state constitutions may offer a third alternative to states that wish to set the gaming rules. However, courts will have to decide whether changing state laws to prohibit, define, or otherwise modify current gaming laws can affect existing state-tribal compacts or negotiations in progress. In 1993, at least three states (Arizona, Idaho, and Wisconsin) acted to prohibit casino-style gaming, either statutorily or by amending their constitutions. Other states moved to approve non-Indian casino operations as the competition for gaming revenues increased. North Dakota approved a study by the Legislative Council in 1995 assessing the future of state-tribal gaming compacts.

The National Indian Gaming Commission has issued definitions that have clarified, to some degree, whether certain gaming devices are categorized as Class II or Class III gaming. Class III devices are subject to compact negotiations rather than falling under Class II tribal jurisdiction, thereby removing one of the contested issues in compact negotiations. The permitted number of Class III machines remains a sticking point in many discussions.

The negotiating process for state-tribal gaming compacts described under IGRA has failed to provide the answer to an important question: Which gambling policy will prevail within a state's boundaries—the one authorized for state citizens by the state legislature or the state constitution or the one(s) on Indian lands that tribes pursue under the federal policy of tribal self-government and self-determination?

The Western Governors' Association and the National Association of Attorneys General have recommended amendments to IGRA. The National Conference of State Legislatures has recommended that IGRA clarify the scope of permitted gaming while respecting compacts that have already been signed. On April 1, 1993, the U.S. House Interior Committee began oversight hearings on Indian gaming issues. The U.S. Senate Committee on Indian Affairs began a series of informal discussions with state and tribal officials. The proposed amendments to IGRA that resulted from those discussions ultimately received no support from either states or tribes. In mid-1995, new amendments were introduced in the

Senate and the House. The new proposals are certain to be controversial. Congress may indeed amend IGRA, but when and how remains to be seen.

Litigation

Litigation also affects the direction of tribal gaming. Federal courts are giving mixed messages to states and tribes about Indian gaming questions. For instance, the federal Ninth Circuit Court of Appeals recently held that IGRA does not require a state to negotiate a gaming activity simply because it has legalized another, though similar, form of gaming. [*Rumsey Indian Rancheria vs. Governor Peter Wilson*, 1994] The court reversed a lower court decision that said California should negotiate with Indian tribes for slot machines and banked card games because California permits and promotes certain other similar forms of gaming. The federal appeals court rejected this analysis, finding that, under IGRA, a state need only allow Indian tribes to operate games that others can operate, but need not give tribes what others cannot have, agreeing with a decision of the Eighth Circuit Court of Appeals in *Cheyenne River Sioux vs. South Dakota*.

The federal appeals court also rejected the premise that Indian tribes may rely on the Supreme Court's decision in *California vs. Cabazon Band* (1987), under which tribes argued they were entitled to offer even gaming prohibited by state law because the state regulated gaming in general, permitting some and prohibiting other forms of gaming. The federal appeals court has indicated that Congress did not intend such a test to apply for Class III gaming under IGRA. Instead, says the court, Congress provided a clear statutory standard: The tribes may negotiate for those gaming activities that are permitted by the state. As such, the *Rumsey* decision, like *Cheyenne River Sioux*, stands for the notion that IGRA is "game specific" when it comes to negotiating for Class III gaming.

Tribes, given the go-ahead under IGRA to sue states for failure to negotiate or failure to negotiate "in good faith," have taken states to court for lack of good faith when negotiations bogged down. Some states have defended themselves from these tribal suits by invoking the 10th and 11th Amendments of the U.S. Constitution. The 10th Amendment states, "The powers not delegated to the United States by the Constitution, nor prohibited by it to the states, are reserved to the states respectively, or to the people." The 11th Amendment states, "The judicial power of the United States shall not be construed to extend to any suit in law or equity, commenced or prosecuted against one of the United States by citizens of another state, or by citizens or subjects of any foreign state." These defenses have been upheld in some courts but not in others, and the Supreme Court has yet to rule on any of the cases involving these issues as they relate to gaming. The courts currently are split regarding claims of states that they are immune from IGRA suits under the 11th Amendment or that the 10th Amendment makes unconstitutional any obligation that the compact process may impose on the states. The Ninth Circuit rejected the state of Washington's claim of 11th Amendment immunity in *Spokane Tribe vs. Washington*. The U.S. Supreme Court agreed on Jan. 23, 1995, to hear *Seminole Tribe of Florida vs. State of Florida* to clarify the question of whether, under the Indian Commerce Clause, Congress had the power when enacting IGRA to abrogate the states' 11th Amendment immunity and subject them to suits by tribes. This is the first tribal gaming case to reach the Supreme Court.

The Future of Tribal Gaming

Negotiating the conduct of tribal gambling activities under IGRA provides states and tribes with a significant opportunity to identify and cooperate on matters of common concern that affect residents in communities where gambling takes place. IGRA's parameters are still being tested, however. To date, the only clear message from court decisions on state challenges to tribal gaming is that tribes may not engage in gaming activities that states specifically prohibit by law—unless the state agrees to such tribal activity. In general, a tribe may engage in Class III gaming in any state that allows such gaming, but a state-tribal compact must be in place before the tribe can proceed with it. Otherwise, the tribe will be in violation of federal law.

A significant question, important to both states and tribes, is the question of sovereignty, both state and tribal. How will the Supreme Court answer the questions created under IGRA? Will Congress change IGRA to clarify its intent? If it does, will Congress specify that tribes must abide by state-established limits? Or will the states be excluded entirely from a role in Indian gaming regulation?

There is little doubt that gaming activities will continue to have a significant impact on evolving state-tribal legal relationships. In 1994, consumers spent 8 percent of their gambling dollars in tribal establishments. Gambling is an emotional issue. Tribally controlled gambling can mean economic survival to tribes that have not found any other successful approach until now. But tribal gambling that conflicts significantly with state law and state policy is bound to be challenged in many states. The most successful states and tribes will be those that can maneuver successfully through the ambiguities of IGRA by acknowledging one another's legitimate concerns and forging gambling regulatory arrangements that benefit all the people of the states and tribes involved.

References

Gaming Developments Bulletin (National Association of Attorneys General), various issues in 1994 and 1995.

Greenberg, Pam, and Judy Zelio. "States and the Indian Gaming Regulatory Act." *NCSL State Legislative Report* (July 1992).

Zelio, Judy. "The Fat New Buffalo." *State Legislatures* 20, no. 6 (June 1994): 38-43.

7. Seeking Agreement on Taxes

Taxation is a controversial issue in state-tribal affairs. State governments and tribal governments both need revenues to provide services to their citizens. They may impose similar taxes on the same economic activities or entities. Enterprises located on some tribal lands may pay less in taxes than similar enterprises on nontribal lands. Tribes and their members are exempt from some taxes that other citizens must pay. Tribal businesses are not required to pay some taxes that nontribal businesses pay. These are some of the issues that can lead to discontent and disputes that sometimes stretch into multi-year lawsuits, strained relationships, and loss of income for both governments. On the positive side, a number of states and tribes have created cooperative relationships that relieve some of these difficulties.

This chapter discusses taxation as it applies to individual Native Americans, Indian tribes, and non-Indians doing business on tribal lands and concludes with examples of state-tribal tax agreements. Definitive statements about Indian taxation are difficult to make, and the findings in one set of circumstances cannot always be applied to another. As a result, this discussion is very general and should be viewed with caution since generalizations can be misleading. For specifics and references, readers may want to consult other sources listed in the resource list. Most useful are Felix Cohen's *Handbook of Federal Indian Law* (1972), Getches and Wilkinson's *Federal Indian Law* (1986), and Pevar's *The Rights of Indians and Tribes* (ACLU), as well as recent case law. Information in the sections called "Federal Taxes" and "State Taxes" is based on Erickson and Martin's 1992 report to the Montana Legislative Council, *Taxation on Indian Reservations*.

Raising Revenues Through Taxes and Fees

Federal funds directed to tribes represent the national government's commitment to historical treaty and trust responsibilities to those tribes. However, the national government, under growing pressure to cut spending, has appeared increasingly eager for tribes to assume a greater share of the costs of reservation services as well as administrative responsibilities. Tribal governments traditionally have been reluctant to levy taxes on their members because of general hostility to taxation and the extensive poverty that exists on many Indian reservations, but some tribes are assuming heavier burdens of social and educational services and are making correspondingly greater efforts to raise revenues through taxes and fees. The resulting competition among states and tribes for scarce revenues raises questions about rights and responsibilities that often have very complicated answers.

Taxes on Indian People

Federal law and treaties limit Native Americans' tax liability, although they still are subject to a variety of state and federal taxes. Individual Indians pay the same taxes as other citizens with the following exceptions: (1) they do not pay federal income tax on income derived from trust lands held for them by the United States; (2) they do not pay state income tax on income earned on a federal reservation (with some exceptions); (3) they do not pay state sales taxes on transactions occurring on a federal reservation; and (4) generally they do not pay local property taxes on reservation or trust land, although local governments may tax and zone some Indian individuals' (but not tribes') property under some circumstances [*County of Yakima vs. Confederated Tribes and Bands of the Yakima Indian Nation*, 112 S. Ct. 683, 1992].

Generally, the application of federal tax laws to Indians and tribes is dependent on interpreting the purposes of treaties, Indian laws, and tax laws. For instance, federal tax laws may not infringe on the treaty rights of Indians or on Indian legislation, unless there is congressional intent to the contrary. State powers to tax are very limited on Indian lands and particularly so when Indian economic interests are affected.

Federal Taxes

Federal income and employment taxes for employers. Like other governments, Indian tribes are not taxable entities under the income tax provisions of the federal Internal Revenue Code.

Tribes are, however, subject to federal employment taxation in three areas: Social Security (FICA), unemployment compensation (FUTA), and withholding for individual income taxes. Indian tribes acting as employers are subject to all three, except for compensation paid for services performed by tribal council members. (The exemption for payments to council members is based on the definition of "wages" in the withholding statute that excludes "fees paid to a public official.")

The Internal Revenue Service has ruled that federal employment taxes apply to Indian tribes, but the applicability of FICA and FUTA statutes is still unclear. Those statutes contain exemptions for certain employer classes either by a specific exemption or by exclusion from the definition of "American employer." Neither FICA nor FUTA makes specific mention of Indians or tribes, even in their legislative histories. However, both FICA and FUTA have broad purposes of providing coverage for all employees. Therefore, whether or not FICA and FUTA taxes apply to Indian tribes remains questionable. until determined by the courts.

FUTA may raise jurisdictional concerns because the tax is administered by the states and because benefits are paid under state plans. Application of FUTA to Indian individuals living on reservations also raises jurisdictional issues. Indian employers that wish to provide coverage to their employees pay the state tax.

Federal excise taxes. In 1983, Congress amended the Internal Revenue Code to treat Indian tribal governments as states for certain purposes relating to taxation, including exemptions from certain excise taxes. The Tribal Tax Status Act of 1982 [P. L. No. 97-473, 96 Stat. 2607] exempts tribal governments from tax on purchases of items such as gasoline and other fuel oil products, communications equipment, and firearms, as well as from certain highway use taxes. If a tribe does pay tax on fuel, the tribe may use the same refund and credit provisions that state and local governments use.

Federal individual income taxes. Individual income of Indians associated with the trust relationship between Indians and the United States generally is exempt from federal income tax. This is income from individually allotted land that remains in trust and income that is payment resulting from judgments against the United States based on claims for land takings or unfair dealings.

However, not all income derived from allotted land is tax-exempt. To be exempt, the income must be derived directly from the property, e.g., rents, royalties or sales of crops, livestock, or minerals. Income as the result of use of capital improvements on allotted land may be taxable. Other types of income that are taxable include exempt income that is reinvested, income from land removed from trust and for which a fee patent is issued, and income from trust land leased from a tribe by an individual tribal member.

Indian allotments that are exempt from income tax, along with accumulated income derived from allotments, are exempt from estate tax. Because of a lack of cases or rulings on gift taxation, it is presumed that the same principles covering estate taxation apply to the taxation of gifts of allotted or other trust property.

Individual Indians—as employers and employees—are subject to federal employment tax laws, such as Social Security and withholding of unemployment tax, and to federal income tax.

Federal excise taxes. Generally speaking, individual Indians pay federal excise taxes.

State Taxes

Outside the boundaries of a reservation, Indian people are subject to the same state tax laws that apply to other state citizens, unless a federal law or treaty confers a special immunity, or unless a state grants exemptions. States have some powers to tax on reservations, but these powers are limited. The state may not tax when:

- the subject matter is preempted by federal law, or
- the tax would infringe upon the right of reservation Indians to make their own laws and be governed by them.

State income taxes. States may not tax the income of tribal members who live and work on their tribe's reservation, but states may tax the income of tribal members who live and work off the reservation. States also may impose taxes on income and nontrust property of Indian individuals who are not members of the tribe on whose reservation they work and reside. States may tax non-Indians' income earned on a reservation.

State sales and use taxes. States may tax sales to and by non-Indians on tribal lands, but they may not tax sales to and by tribal members when the transaction occurs on tribal or trust lands. Non-Indians are liable for state taxes on purchases they make on Indian lands, and tribes are obligated to help collect validly imposed state taxes on such sales. However, tribes are immune from suit by the state. See *Oklahoma Tax Comm'n vs. Citizen Band Potawatomi Indian Tribe of Okla.*, 498 U.S. 505 (1991). Indian people are liable for state sales taxes on transactions conducted off reservation lands. Idaho exempts sales of tangible personal property within Idaho Indian reservations if a business is wholly owned and operated by a state-recognized Indian tribe [Sec. 63-3622Z]. Mississippi exempts sales to the Mississippi Band of Choctaw Indians but not sales to Indians individually [Sec. 27-65-105]. It also exempts sales on reservation lands of the Mississippi Band of Choctaw Indians if tribal sales tax is paid [Sec. 27-65-213]. Texas exempts purchases by the Alabama-Coushatta Indian Tribe, the Tigua Indian Tribe, and the Texas Band of Kickapoo Indians, as well as sales of items made by members of such tribes and cultural artifacts of the tribe sold within reservation boundaries or on trust land held by the tribe [Tax Code, Sec. 151.337].

Retail outlets located on Indian lands and operated by tribes (or in some cases Indian individuals) sometimes offer products—especially gasoline and cigarettes whose price elsewhere includes state excise taxes—at lower prices than non-Indian businesses can sell them, creating a competitive advantage for Indian retailers. Sales of this nature can generate tax revenue losses for states. Although in most states non-Indian buyers are supposed to pay taxes on these retail purchases, in reality they do not do so unless the Indian retailers agree to cooperate with state officials. Some states and tribes have agreements in place to work on these issues.

Property taxes. State and local governments have the power to levy taxes on most property owned by non-Indians within a reservation. Land owned in fee by individual Indian people usually is also subject to property taxation. Most land owned by tribes and land held in trust by the federal government is not taxable. Federal impact aid to school districts with Indian students may compensate for some forgone property tax revenue.

Severance taxes. States may levy taxes on firms doing business on Indian lands even though a tribe may be imposing a similar tax, resulting in double taxation. [*Cotton Petroleum Corp. vs. New Mexico*, 490 U.S. 163 (1989)].

State and Tribal Taxation

Tribes in some instances have argued that a tribal tax upon an activity should preempt a state from taxing the same activity. If the tribal tax has regulatory purposes that are hindered by a state tax, the state tax may be invalid if it interferes with tribal self-government. However, the Supreme Court has said that the mere existence of a tribal tax does not invalidate a state tax even when the result is double taxation [*Washington vs. Confederated Tribes of Colville Indian Reservation*, 447 U.S. 134 (1980) and *Cotton Petroleum Corporation vs. New Mexico*, 490 U.S. 163 (1989)].

Generally, taxes imposed by tribes fall on non-Indians who are engaging in economic activity on Indian lands, frequently natural resource extraction. Taxes on cigarettes and utilities and a possessory interest (leasehold) tax also are levied by different tribes. When a tribe and a state seek to tax and regulate the same activity, significant problems may be created, according to Douglas Endreson, author of *Resolving Tribal-State Tax Conflicts*, including the economic impacts of regulatory confusion, inefficiency, and double taxation.

Double taxation. Businesses subject to taxation by both state and tribal governments may decide to locate where only one government levies taxes (although extractive industries are not always so portable). Such location decisions may slow or halt economic development on Indian lands and in surrounding areas, causing both state and tribal governments to lose potential revenue—from severance, income, and sales taxes, for example. States and tribes have considered various solutions: The state may give up its claim to tax in favor of the tribal tax in order to support tribal economic development. The tribe and state may find ways to improve both parties' ability to collect taxes through increased enforcement efforts. The tribe and state may agree on formulas to split the revenues that one tax would generate.

State-Tribal Tax Conflict Resolution

Conflicts over imposing state taxes on reservation sales to non-Indians have been dealt with between tribes and states in several locations. States where agreements have been concluded include Maine, Minnesota, Montana, Oklahoma, Oregon, South Dakota, Utah, and Wisconsin. Several other states, including New Mexico, Kansas, North Dakota, and Washington, are in the process of attempting to negotiate such agreements. A number of states with sizable Indian populations have no tax agreements in place, including Arizona, Colorado, Idaho, and New York. New York has explored such agreements in the past with the Seneca Nation and may continue to do so because a recent U.S. Supreme Court decision upheld a state law that requires special recordkeeping and quantity limitations on untaxed cigarettes sold by wholesalers to reservation Indians. [*Department of Taxation and Finance of the State of New York vs. Milhelm Attea and Bros. Inc.* 114 S.Ct. 2028 (1994)]

A tribal government must see a need for a stable source of revenue that an agreement can help provide, points out Harley Duncan, director of the Federation of Tax Administrators. Otherwise, there is no reason for a tribal government to enter into an agreement that would increase the price of goods and services sold by the tribe or its agents.

The state, on the other hand, says Duncan, should recognize that its best interests may lie in not collecting all the state tax due on sales to nontribal members. There may be considerable value in ensuring that all citizens comply with state tax laws, regardless of who receives the revenue. There is also value in reducing the competitive disadvantage faced by nontribal retailers who compete with tribal retailers, even though the state may not receive the tax revenues. States that examine the state-tribal tax issue as an economic question rather than a purely legal one could find their overall interests served by a tax-sharing arrangement, with a portion of the proceeds from sales to nontribal members shared with the tribal government.

State Statutes and Regulations as a Means of Resolving Tax Conflicts

Several states have addressed state-tribal tax issues through legislation and regulations, and the following section provides illustrative examples. To date, most of the arrangements have involved cigarette or other tobacco taxes, but a few extend to other taxes as well.

Florida. In 1977 Florida enacted a statute that exempted from state taxation all cigarette sales on Seminole land [Fla. Stat. 210.05(5)]. The Seminole Tribe imposed and collected a tax higher than the state tax on cigarette sales, reporting that sales remained competitive because of the tribal vendors' low overhead and subsidized prices from the tribally owned wholesaler to the vendors.

Mississippi. In 1986 Mississippi enacted a statute under which it relinquished any jurisdiction to collect sales or gross receipts taxes within reservation lands of the Mississippi Band of Choctaw Indians when the vendor was authorized to do business on the reservation by the tribe and was paying the tribal sales tax [Miss. Code Ann. 27-65-215 (1986)].

Montana. In 1993 Montana enacted legislation to address state cigarette taxation within reservation boundaries. Sales by retailers to members of a tribe on whose reservation the sales occur are subject to an annually determined quota of tax-free cigarettes. Quotas may be determined either by cooperative agreement between the tribes and the state, or by statute. Taxes are collected from wholesalers before sale to retailers. The wholesalers then may apply to the state for a refund or credit. The total amount of refunds or credits to all wholesalers may not exceed an amount equal to the tax due on the quota allocation [Sec. 16-11-111].

Nevada. In 1991, Nevada passed legislation allowing refunds for state tax paid on tobacco products other than cigarettes sold to any person on a reservation where an excise tax equal to or greater than the Nevada tax was imposed [Ch. 6990, Laws 1991]. Legislation also established that the governing body of an Indian reservation could impose an excise tax on any cigarettes sold on the reservation [Ch. 269, Laws 1991; Sec. 370.501]. The state Department of Taxation will not collect the tax if the governing body of the reservation imposes an excise tax under state authorizing provisions; the excise tax is equal to or greater than the state tax rate on cigarette or tobacco products; and the tribal government submits a copy of the imposing ordinance to the state revenue department [Sec. 370.515].

New Mexico. In 1992, the state exempted from cigarette taxation cigarettes sold to the tribal governing body or to any enrolled tribal member licensed by the governing body of any Indian nation, tribe, or pueblo for use or sale on that reservation or pueblo [Ch. 37, Laws 1992, Sec. 7-12-4].

Oklahoma. In 1992, the state passed legislation designed to help collect tobacco taxes on sales to non-Indians in tribally owned stores. The law imposes on tribal sales a payment in lieu of taxes equal to 75 percent of state cigarette and tobacco excise taxes due, and outlines a plan under which tribes that agree to regulate sales (including application of stamps) and enter into compacts with the state make payments in lieu of taxes equal to only 25 percent of the excise taxes due [S.B. 759, Laws 1992, Tit. 68, Sec. 321, 1355].

Washington. Washington requires that vendors collect cigarette taxes on cigarettes sold by Indians to non-Indians [Wash. Admin. Code R. 458-20-192 (1985)]; that is, the cigarette tax is paid with stamps purchased from the Department of Revenue by the first person who sells, uses, consumes, handles, possesses, or distributes the cigarettes. The stamps must be attached to each package [Sec. 82.24.090]. Wholesalers who furnish a surety bond may set aside, without stamps, stocks of cigarettes for sales to approved Indian tribal organizations [Sec. 82.23.040]. Indian vendors must obtain a stamped supply of cigarettes for sale to non-Indians [Wash. Admin. Code R. 458-2-192]. Indians may purchase unstamped cigarettes only for resale to qualified purchasers, that is, Indians [Wash. Admin. Code R. 458-20-192]. Wholesalers of cigarettes must furnish to the Department of Revenue duplicate invoices of shipments to Indian tribal organizations [Sec. 82.24.090].

Wisconsin. Cigarette taxes also are precollected in Wisconsin, [Wis. Stat. 139.31(1) (1987)]. The tax is imposed at the time and place of the first taxable event and then is passed on to the consumer [Wis. Stat. 139.31(1) (1987)]. Tribes receive 70 percent of the taxes generated by reservation cigarette sales if five conditions are met: (1) the tribal council must file a claim for the refund with the Department of Revenue; (2) the cigarette retailer must be approved by the tribal council; (3) the land on which the sale occurred must have been reservation or trust land on or before January 1, 1983; (4) the cigarettes must not be delivered by a retailer to a buyer by way of common carrier, contract carrier, or the U.S. Postal Service; and (5) the retailer must not have sold cigarettes to another retailer or jobber [(Wis. Stat. 139.323 (1987)]. Wis. Stat. 139.325 also authorizes the Department of Revenue to enter into cigarette tax refund agreements with Indian tribes with regard to cigarettes sold on reservations to enrolled tribal members.

Tax Agreements Entered Into by Tribes and States

A state-tribal tax agreement is an arrangement between two governments that addresses specific jurisdictional issues in taxation. State-tribal agreements require government-to-government discussion between tribal and state officials. Such discussions allow tribal and state leaders to talk directly and specifically about revenue needs, economic development objectives, and the practical, political, and economic concerns that arise from tax conflicts. This approach—unlike litigation—enables the tribe and the state, not a court, to decide whether results are satisfactory.

Each state must consider whether a specific statutory enactment is necessary for the lawful creation of such agreements, and a separate agreement with each tribal government is needed. If a tax conflict is to be resolved, both the tribe and the state must assent to the terms of any agreements. Agreements may not be possible with all tribes within a state's borders.

Joel Michael of the Minnesota House of Representatives Research Department points out that agreements between tribes and states may be generated as a result of two difficulties in particular: the impracticality of state collection of state tax legally owed by non-Indians for transactions in Indian country, and the potential for illegally imposing state tax on immune tribal members or businesses. Minnesota, for example, has tax agreements with 10 different tribes, which use formulas to determine refunds to tribes from sales and motor vehicle excise taxes, cigarette taxes, alcoholic beverage taxes, and petroleum taxes. The agreements attempt to preserve the tribes' and tribal members' immunity while collecting the state tax legally owed by non-tribal members. Other states and tribes also have reached state-tribal agreements that illustrate a variety of approaches to these difficulties.

Tax compact between Louisiana and the Chitimacha Tribe. In 1990, Louisiana and the Chitimacha Tribe entered into a tax compact under which the state acknowledges that the tribe is exempt from assessment of certain state sales and use taxes and agrees not to collect two types of taxes from the tribe: (1) sales and use taxes on tribally owned motor vehicles and (2) cigarette and tobacco taxes on reservation sales of cigarettes and tobacco products. Other tax issues are left either for further agreements or for judicial resolution.

Agreement between Nevada and the Reno Sparks Tribe. A 1991 tax agreement between Nevada and the Reno Sparks Tribe provides that the tribe may impose an excise tax on tobacco products sold and a sales tax on retail sales on the reservation. The state agrees that it will not impose sales and excise taxes on on-reservation sales of cigarettes or tangible personal property if two conditions are met: (1) the tribe adopts a tax ordinance and files it with the state and (2) the tax imposed by the tribe is greater than or equal to the taxes that the state would impose. The tribes also agree not to price cigarettes or tobacco products below wholesale cost plus the tax. The agreement contains specific provisions to deal with off-reservation tribal businesses and non-Indian contractors. Further, the tribe agrees that the state cigarette and sales taxes would apply to tribal and Indian businesses operating outside of the reservations.

Agreement between Montana and the Fort Peck and Assiniboine Sioux Tribes. In April 1992 the Montana Department of Revenue and the Fort Peck Tribes concluded a cigarette tax agreement calling for establishment of a maximum annual quota of 60,000 cartons of cigarettes to be sold tax-free on the Fort Peck Reservation. The tribes agree to license retailers entitled to receive quota cigarettes. The tribes also agree to adopt and enforce an ordinance prohibiting untaxed cigarette sales to people on the reservation not entitled to buy the cigarettes tax-free. Native American retailers are expected to keep detailed records of all sales of quota cigarettes.

Agreements between New Mexico and the Pueblos of Santa Clara and Pojoaque. New Mexico and the pueblos are working on the development of a unified tax collection system that will allow shared revenues. The governments have agreed to coordinate collection of gross receipts taxes.

Agreements between Oklahoma and the Cherokee Nation. Oklahoma and the Cherokee Nation (as well as four other tribes) signed agreements in June 1992. Under the agreements, the tribes and their licensees agree to make in-lieu-of-tax payments to the state equal to 25 percent of all applicable excise taxes. All cigarettes sold must carry tribal and state stamps or a single stamp approved by both parties, verifying that applicable tribal taxes and payments in lieu of state taxes were paid to the wholesaler at the time of purchase. Both parties agree that unstamped cigarettes are contraband and that each party has the right to seize contraband within its boundaries [Tribal/State Tobacco Tax Compact filed June 8, 1992, with the Oklahoma Secretary of State]. Tribes without compacts are assessed in-lieu taxes equal to 75 percent of the regular excise taxes due on cigarettes and tobacco products.

Agreement between the Warm Springs Confederated Tribes and the Oregon Department of Revenue. A 1979 agreement between Oregon and the Warm Springs Tribal Council provides for the state and tribe to share revenues generated by tribal collection of the state tax on cigarettes. The amount of the tribe's share, which the state refunds, is computed under a formula by which the per capita cigarette consumption, the number of enrolled tribal members, and the current tax rate are multiplied.

Agreements between South Dakota and the Standing Rock Sioux, Rosebud Sioux, Cheyenne River Sioux, and Oglala Sioux Tribes. Four tribes have entered into tax agreements with South Dakota: the Oglala Sioux in 1971, the Cheyenne River Sioux Tribe in 1977, the Rosebud Sioux Tribe in 1978, and the Standing Rock Sioux Tribe in 1991. The collection agreements provide for the state to administer and collect the state sales, use, and cigarette and tobacco taxes as well as parallel tribal taxes identical to the state taxes. There is no double taxation. The state and tribes agree to a percentage split of the collections on each reservation, based on Indian/non-Indian population figures. In 1991, the Oglala Sioux received 91 percent ($475,000) of collections, the Cheyenne River Sioux 58 percent ($420,000), the Rosebud Sioux 75 percent ($722,000), and the Standing Rock Sioux 47 percent ($31,000). The state deducts a 1 percent administrative fee from the tribal proceeds to cover expenses; the tribal portion of the tax receipts is sent to the tribes every two weeks.

Summary

Tax revenues are essential to the operation of government, the delivery of services, and the development of infrastructure. Tribal governments are just beginning to exercise their taxing authority as an aid to achieving self-determination and economic self-sufficiency. As a result, conflicts occur between states and tribes as they compete for tax revenue from the same sources, either from non-Indian businesses operating on a reservation or on transactions between tribal businesses and non-Indians. For many years, these conflicts were resolved by litigation at tremendous costs in time and money for states and tribes.

Some states and tribes are increasingly pursuing options to litigation, the most successful being negotiated agreements. In the negotiation process, both sides can discuss, in a nonadversarial environment, revenue needs, economic development objectives, and economic concerns.

Resources

Black, Anne. *Natural Resource Revenue Sources of Ten Selected Indian Tribes in the Rocky Mountain Region.* Vol. 2 of *For Current and Future Generations.* Billings, Mont.: Western Organization of Resource Councils, June 1989.

Blassman, George A. "New York State's Experience With the Federal Indian Trader Statutes." *State Tax Notes*, August 10, 1992.

Cohen, Felix S. *Handbook of Federal Indian Law, with Reference Tables and Index.* Washington, D.C.: Government Printing Office, 1942. Reprinted, Albuquerque: University of New Mexico Press, 1972.

Consensus. The Public Disputes Network Newsletter. Program on Negotiation at Harvard Law School, Cambridge, Mass., 1990.

Duncan, Harley. "Issues in State-Tribal Taxation." Bulletin B-232, Nov. 21, 1991. Federation of Tax Administrators, Washington, D.C.

Endreson, Douglas B.L. *Resolving Tribal-State Tax Conflicts.* Washington, D.C.: National Indian Policy Center, June 1991.

Erickson, Connie. *Improving State-Tribal Relations: 1991-92 Activities of the Committee on Indian Affairs.* Helena: Montana Legislative Council, November 1992.

Erickson, Connie, and Jeff Martin. *Taxation on Indian Reservations and Other Issues Before the Revenue Oversight Committee.* Helena: Montana Legislative Council, November 1992.

Erickson, Connie, Lois Menzies, and Eddye McClure. *Taxation on Montana Indian Reservations.* Helena: Montana Legislative Council, January 1990.

Getches, David H. "Negotiated Sovereignty: Intergovernmental Agreements with American Indian Tribes as Models for Expanding Self-Government." *Review of Constitutional Studies,* I no. 1, (1993): 161.

Getches, David H., and Charles F. Wilkinson. *Federal Indian Law: Cases and Materials,* 2nd ed. St. Paul, Minn.: West Publishing Co., 1986.

McGown, John. "Indian Taxation in Idaho: The State and Federal Pictures." *State Tax Notes,* April 25, 1994.

Michael, Joel. "Taxation in Indian Country." In *Indians, Indian Tribes and State Government.* St. Paul, Minn.: Research Department, Minnesota House of Representatives, February 1993.

Montana Committee on Indian Affairs (Eddye McClure, Connie Erickson, Stephen Maly, and Susan Byorth Fox, staff*). The Tribal Nations of Montana: A Handbook for Legislators.* Helena: Montana Legislative Council, March 1995.

Novotny, Roger. "South Dakota Splits Tax Revenues with Tribes." *The Fiscal Letter* (National Conference of State Legislatures. September/October 1991).

Pecos, Regis. "Briefing Paper on State/Tribal Jurisdiction Issues as Requested by Ms. Jo Clark, Indian Jurisdiction Project, Western Governors' Association." New Mexico Office of Indian Affairs, Santa Fe, September 22, 1987. Memorandum to Governor Garrey Carruthers of New Mexico.

Pevar, Stephen L. *The Rights of Indians and Tribes: The Basic ACLU Guide to Indian and Tribal Rights,* 2nd ed. Carbondale: Southern Illinois University Press, 1992.

Sullivan, Jeffrey C. "Taxation and Indian Lands," *State Tax Notes,* August 10, 1992.

Taylor, Theodore W. *American Indian Policy.* Mount Airy, Md.: Lomond Publications, Inc., 1983.

Washington State Legislature Legislative Budget Committee. *Cigarette Tax Study,* Report No. 90-2. Olympia, April 27, 1990.

8. NATURAL RESOURCE ALLOCATION AND MANAGEMENT

Natural resource allocation and management have been yet another prime source of conflict between states and tribes, and federal courts have been the main battleground for resolving the disputes. Current controversies over the treatment of resources on Indian land have received tremendous attention. Congress considered approximately 665 related bills between 1990 and 1994, numerous federal reports have been issued, and literally millions of words have been written that address the complex legal, historical, and cultural context of Native American land and natural resource questions. State legislatures have examined hundreds of bills in this area as well. This chapter examines two particular situations that are representative of these types of conflicts: water rights in Idaho and fishing rights in Washington and the ingredients that made for successful agreement. (A good place to start for further, in-depth reading on natural resource conflict is the bibliographic essay by Rennard Strickland and Maria Proffi, "The Dilemma of Preserving Tribal Culture and Promoting Resource Development" in *Natural Resources and Environment*, Spring 1993.)

The past 20 years have been marked by litigation concerning Indian peoples' rights through treaties, statutes, executive orders, and agreements to named, yet formerly unquantified, resources. In 1994 alone, 10 major natural resources decisions were made in federal courts dealing with questions of ownership and use of water, timber, methane, and fish and game. Local Indian and non-Indian residents, private industry, and state, tribal, and federal governments have sought to transform adversarial legal battles into conciliatory agreements. Expanding populations, limited resources, tribal pursuits to foster economic development, state interests in environmental preservation, and assertion of Indian treaty rights challenge both states and Indian tribes to develop responsible and equitable resolutions to centuries-old disputes.

The present condition of state-tribal relations regarding natural resources has evolved from the different phases of Indian policy in the United States. Treaties between the United States and tribes acknowledge the sovereignty of tribes that is exercised in Indian country, defined generally as lands within reservations, dependent Indian communities, and Indian allotments. Much of the litigation of the past 20 years concerning Indian treaty rights involves rights to natural resources such as timber, water, minerals, and gas, as well as hunting, gathering, and fishing in usual and accustomed places. Tribes exercise significant rights on the land controlled and governed by tribes and in lands ceded to the United States that became privately owned. This land base amounts to nearly 53 million acres, or almost 3 percent of land within the borders of the United States.

The culture and very survival of Native American peoples roots itself in the land. As David Getches, professor of law at the University of Colorado, notes: "At the heart of the Native American struggle for tribal existence and self-sufficiency is the need to protect and use natural resources. . . However diverse native cultures may be, they have a common thread: their dependence on the natural world for definition and continuity. And of course Native Americans have always looked to the land for sustenance." The exercise of tribal sovereignty and preservation of cultural identity depend on connection with the land.

Much of the original treaty lands have been ceded, allotted, and sold. Reservations, therefore, tend to be composed of tribal, non-Indian, allotted, and fee lands.

Conflicting Claims to Limited Water Resources

Water is a scarce, and therefore valuable, resource in the western states. The federal government, as a trustee, is required to advance the best interests of the tribes. Yet historically, federal water projects have benefited non-Indian water users, and few funds have been directed to Indian tribes to develop their water resources. Most western rivers are fully claimed, and recognition of Indian water rights jeopardizes the present water users' supply. Resolving conflicting claims is necessary for all parties to plan for the future. It is in states' interest to move away from judicial reallocation decisions to more comprehensive agreements addressing improved water management to benefit all parties.

Western states have used the "prior appropriation" doctrine to allocate water rights. Prior appropriation grants a water user a right that takes precedence over later users if he or she appropriates the water by putting it to beneficial use. Diversion used to be considered a prerequisite, but court decisions and in-stream flow statutes have clarified that a diversion is not necessary (except in New Mexico and possibly Nevada). The 18 western states that subscribe, to varying degrees, to the prior appropriation doctrine tend to define beneficial use to include irrigation, mining, industrial, or domestic uses. Ten states also recognize the maintenance of fish and wildlife habitat as a beneficial use. The water user has "perfected" his or her water right once these conditions (diversion in some states and beneficial use) have been met. Junior water users (those who claim the water at a later time) may use the water available after the senior rights are met. According to the prior appropriation doctrine, a water right must be used or it can be considered abandoned and consequently lost.

Indian Water Rights

Indian water rights are defined by federal rather than state law; thus, Indian-reserved water rights are not determined through the prior appropriation doctrine. The U.S. Supreme Court ruled in the *Winters* case of 1908 that tribes have the right to use sufficient water for present and future needs that fulfill the purposes for which the reservations were established. Those purposes may range from irrigation for agriculture to restoring streams and forests. The priority date of tribal water rights is the date on which the reservation was created regardless of actual water diversion and use by Indians. Therefore, Indian-reserved water rights have priority dates earlier than those of non-Indian uses begun after the establishment of the reservations. Under *Winters*, beneficial use as defined by states is not required in order to maintain Indian-reserved water rights. According to Daniel McCool, "Indian tribes often lagged behind their Anglo neighbors in developing irrigated farming and other beneficial uses of water. This meant that by the time the reservations were ready to put water to use, all sources of water would already have been allocated to non-Indians." The result has been conflict as Indian tribes seek to exercise their water rights.

The State Role in Settling Water Claims

Federal lands constitute 60 percent of the watershed in 11 western states. Conflicts were inevitable between federally reserved water rights defined by the Winters Doctrine and state-granted rights based on prior appropriation. The McCarran Amendment of 1952 reaffirmed congressional intent to respect the supremacy of state law in water administration. The amendment authorizes suit against the United States to ascertain water rights within a river system and requires suits to be comprehensive enough to include all water users in that system. Under the amendment, the United States waives its sovereign immunity and its right to plead that state laws are not applicable.

To include all water users in adjudication, the rights of all claimants to water in a river system or basin must be determined. This has several benefits. Once all rights are ranked and quantified, and uncertainty eliminated, state water management programs may be better able to run effectively and efficiently, and Indian and non-Indian water users may be better able to plan for the future. State courts have jurisdiction over adjudication proceedings because of the supremacy of state law in matters of state water administration. Several western states have been involved in water claims disputes.

Quantifying the senior reserved rights of Indian tribes to determine the quantity of water to which a tribe is entitled is a first step in the adjudication process. Currently, the only standard recognized by the Supreme Court for quantification of Indian reserved water rights in general stream adjudications is "practically irrigable acreage," or PIA. Though other formulas have been used by lower courts, PIA determines the amount of water needed to irrigate all practically irrigable acreage to satisfy present and future agricultural needs. Most Native American tribes object to the quantification of water rights as it places a cap on potentially unlimited tribal water rights and assumes that agricultural irrigation is the purpose for which water will be used. Furthermore, many believe PIA is inequitable between tribes with vastly different land holdings. Yet it is generally understood that quantification is central to identifying the nature and extent of the water needs of Indian reservations and is a pragmatic approach for tribes to develop water needed to serve growing populations and economies.

The Case of Idaho: Settling Water Rights

Examining the development of a state-tribal negotiation process to quantify and administer reserved water rights may help other states avoid costly and lengthy litigation concerning water rights. Fifteen major tribal water settlements were achieved from 1982 to 1992. One such negotiation involved Idaho, the Shoshone-Bannock tribes, certain Idaho water users, and the United States government. The negotiation was initiated prior to litigation and addressed a comprehensive agenda while structuring future cooperative state and tribal administration of water rights. This Fort Hall settlement shows how good faith negotiations, along with innovation and flexibility, can produce an agreement that achieves the primary goals of the negotiating parties.

In 1985, the Idaho Legislature instructed the director of the Department of Water Resources to petition the Idaho Fifth Judicial District Court for a general adjudication of the Snake River Basin. The affected tribes requested the legislature to undertake a negotiated settlement rather than pursue litigation. Personal visits with individual legislators and prior state-tribal work on cigarette taxes helped lay the groundwork for a process of negotiation. Tribal leaders generally favored settling disputes out of court. There was a nearly unanimous vote by the legislature to undertake a negotiated settlement. Legislation included a directive to the state to engage in good faith, government-to-government negotiations with the Shoshone-Bannock tribes and to avoid litigation in determining the extent and nature of the tribes' water rights in the Snake River Basin reserved under the Winters Doctrine.

The state, the federal government, and the tribes worked out one memorandum of understanding in 1985 and another in 1987, which established the negotiation process and a method for reviewing the tribes' water claims. The parties to the eventual settlement, rather than a court-appointed water master, decided how to evaluate Indian water rights. Parties consented that the state court would use the agreement as the legal judgment for tribal water claims without trial or adjudication of fact or law.

Support for the negotiations was widespread. Idaho tribes generally favored negotiation and cooperation even though they had been successful in a number of litigated cases over the previous 15 years. Indian attorneys and leaders were wary of decisions by an increasingly conservative Supreme Court that showed less sympathy for Indian interests. Also, negotiating water rights ensures that "wet" water is delivered instead of relying on "paper" rights that may be larger but are eventually useless unless the tribe has the money to develop them. The Bureau of Indian Affairs and the Justice Department agreed that the Shoshone-Bannock tribes would participate on their own behalf in the negotiations. The governor of Idaho issued executive orders stating that it was in the state's interest to settle through negotiated agreements all claims for water rights reserved under federal law.

The agreement reached through negotiation included the allocation of 581,031 acre feet of water per year to the Shoshone-Bannock tribes of the Fort Hall Reservation to be used for irrigation, domestic, commercial, municipal, industrial, and livestock uses. Water also may be used by the tribes to enhance in-stream flows and to develop hydropower projects. The agreement recognizes the unlimited right to market water on the reservation and a limited, yet significant, right to market water off the reservation. The negotiated agreement coordinates tribal and state administration of water rights to protect Indian and non-Indian interests. Furthermore, it protects present water users and provides for contributions by federal and state governments. It creatively involved federal storage rights, held in trust for the tribes, to provide water when Snake River flows diminished. The priority date assigned to the reservation's water right was June 14, 1867, the date the reservation was created.

The tentative settlement, titled the Fort Hall Indian Water Rights Act of 1990, was passed Oct. 10, 1990. It directed the Interior Department to provide storage space in some federal reservoirs to "specified nonfederal interests; forgive certain outstanding obligations to repay the federal government for the construction of that storage space; and provide for the use of water by the tribes." The act also authorized $22 million to be appropriated over three years to establish a tribal development fund, construct water management systems for the reservation, and acquire land and grazing rights. Traditional tribal values were recognized in the settlement by allowing water use for fish, wildlife, and environmental purposes, in addition to agriculture.

The Idaho Legislature and the Shoshone-Bannock Tribal Council ratified the negotiated settlement in 1991. The Fifth Judicial Court of Idaho approved the 1990 Fort Hall Indian Water Rights Agreement on Aug. 2, 1995. The parties to the settlement accomplished more than an agreement through negotiation; they developed methods of future water administration and a working relationship between the state and tribes that minimized the adversary nature of water rights litigation. This agreement addressed the tough questions of new water development, costs of settlement, and water marketing that have often tied up other water disputes.

The Case of Washington: Developing Joint Fishery Management

Both Indians and non-Indians have an interest in integrated fish and game management to protect common resources. Environmental programs implemented by tribes in cooperation with state and federal government re-establish habitat and protect fish and wildlife used by sportsmen, the tribe, and recreational interests. Yet state regulations that aim at preserving the resource can conflict with tribal fishing and hunting rights and result in bitter disputes.

**A Case of Cooperation: The Confederated Tribes of the
Umatilla Reservation and Umatilla County**

The Confederated Tribes of the Umatilla reservation in Oregon have developed a vision statement to achieve economic self-sufficiency by the year 2040. The statement stresses the importance of cooperation between the state, the county, and tribes that draws on a county-tribal relationship established over twenty years ago. At that time, non-Indians were attracted to the reservation for its cheap land and lack of zoning. The tribes feared the loss of prime agricultural land to residential development and began to work with the county to coordinate planning efforts. An interim zoning ordinance was adopted in 1973, and a comprehensive plan went into effect in 1979.

Uncertainty remained as to who had jurisdiction over parcels of land on the reservation owned by non-Indians. The county took the question to the state attorney general who ruled that the Umatilla tribes had the authority to impose their regulations concerning land use on non-Indian lands within the reservation. After the Supreme Court confused the issue of jurisdiction in its *Brendale vs. Yakima* ruling, the tribes and the county signed a memorandum of understanding upholding the Umatillas' jurisdiction over all lands on their reservation. Tribal provisions include protection of agriculture, concentrated development, and protection of a subsistence zone used by the Indians for hunting elk and gathering roots.

County-tribal cooperation has resulted in a working relationship beneficial to both parties. The county's planning staff has a reduced workload because of their relationship with the tribes. Cooperative projects include a countywide rural addressing system, emergency preparedness training, and field fire permits. A recent joint venture involved local waste problems. The tribes created a task force in 1989 to study alternatives to their landfill and, after meeting with neighboring town councils, decided to build a waste transfer station on the reservation.

Richard Du Bey, an attorney who represents many tribal governments and organizations, says, "In arguing about who has jurisdiction, the resource generally suffers." States that have experienced conflict with hunting and fishing rights include Oregon, Wisconsin, Minnesota, and Washington.

Washington has a history of fishing rights disputes but recently has succeeded in transforming conflict into cooperation. State-tribal management of salmon fisheries has benefited the resource and its human users.

State-tribal cooperation did not seem possible amid the disputes and confrontations between Indian and non-Indian fishermen in the 1960s and 1970s in Washington. For 75 years after statehood, the State Department of Fisheries (regulating salmon) and the State Department of Game (regulating steelhead trout) told Native Americans they had to follow the same rules as other citizens regarding fishing seasons, locations, and methods. Tribes and the state government disputed fishing rights in the courts as often as 70 times a year. The conflict centered on Indian use of traditional nets to catch steelhead trout. The state had declared steelhead a game fish, to be caught by line and hook. The state resource management plan, including fishing regulations, aimed to halt the decline in fish stocks. The tribes claimed exemption from the regulations due to treaty provisions and the Supremacy Clause in the U.S. Constitution. Indian fishermen, fish and game officers, and local and state police faced each other in confrontation that at times turned violent.

Indian Treaty Fishing Rights

Indian tribes in Washington Territory had signed treaties in 1854 and 1855, the Stevens Treaties, that ceded more than 100,000 square miles of land to white settlers. In return, tribes received monetary payments and government recognition of certain reserved rights. These rights included land for the exclusive use of tribes (reservations) and traditional fishing rights. Indians reserved the right to fish for salmon at "all usual and accustomed grounds and stations . . . in common with all citizens of the territory." Salmon and steelhead trout in the Pacific Northwest served as a trading commodity, a food source, and the focal point for Indian culture. Federal recognition of tribal hunting and fishing rights insulates these particular Indian rights from state laws. The Supremacy Clause asserts that states are prohibited from amending or abrogating federal treaty provisions. Twenty tribes on Puget Sound and in the Olympic Coast area have officially been recognized as signers of treaties.

Provisions of the Stevens Treaties guaranteeing the tribes' reserved rights to fish were soon forgotten in the wake of several developments. New fishing devices that increased the catch of non-Indian fishermen, increased demand for salmon as a result of new canning techniques, and state laws all supported a severe imbalance of catches by non-Indians. By 1970, non-Indian commercial and sport fishermen accounted for 95 percent of catches, and non-Indians owned more than 99 percent of commercial fishing licenses. Urbanization, logging activities, water pollution from sewage and agricultural fertilizers, and dams built on the Columbia River system for electricity caused the harvestable fish supply to dwindle in the Pacific Northwest.

Litigation and the Boldt Decision

Tribes began filing lawsuits to reclaim lost rights, but their legal efforts won little. The period from 1965 to 1973 was marked by intense conflict including harassment of Indian fishermen, violence, and arrests. The federal government filed suit on behalf of 20 Washington tribes before federal District Judge George Boldt in *U.S. vs. Washington* in 1971. The three-year inquiry resulted in reaffirmation of treaty fishing rights and establishment of state-tribal co-management of the resource. The Boldt Decision, issued in February 1974, defined the treaty right to take fish "in common with all citizens of the territory" to mean sharing equally. Treaty tribes were entitled to half of the harvestable return of salmon and steelhead at their off-reservation sites. This right is second only to conservation of the salmon.

Despite the legal ruling, the state of Washington resisted recognition of treaty Indian fishing rights. The state challenged the tribes in court until 1983 to avoid implementing the federal court rulings. Resistance and defiance of the ruling were widespread. The question reached the U.S. Supreme Court eight times, the last time in 1979 in the case *Washington vs. Washington State Commercial Passenger Fishing Vessel Association*. The Supreme Court upheld the substance of the Boldt Decision, including the 50/50 apportionment ruling, and defined this share as a maximum allocation.

Because of the conflict between the state and tribes, the court took over management of the fishery resource by default. Judge Boldt appointed a special master to decide harvest seasons, numbers, and shares, as well as other management questions.

Phase II of *U.S. vs. Washington*

As struggles following the Boldt Decision continued, Judge William Orrick addressed two issues overlooked by Boldt. Orrick determined that tribes have rights to catch hatchery-bred fish and treaties include an implicit right to have fish habitat protected from destruction. Orrick's ruling, known as Phase II of *U.S. vs. Washington*, made it clear that treaties provide an environmental protection right for the tribes.

Declining salmon harvests coupled with new state leadership began the process of conflict resolution. The Department of Fisheries (DOF) new director, Bill Wilkerson, decided in 1982 to attempt discussions rather than continue the incessant litigation. Governor John Spellman agreed to back him, and the state hired a mediator for the first meeting of the Fisheries Department and tribes at Port Ludlow. Wilkerson declared an end to the fish war in 1983, but resistance continued. Opponents of the Boldt Decision presented a statewide ballot initiative to invalidate treaty rights and won 53 percent of the vote. The initiative never took effect because of the supremacy of federally recognized Indian treaties over state law, but it indicated the hostile environment in which the talks at Port Ludlow began.

As state and tribal representatives met at Port Ludlow, they shared a frustration with the ongoing situation and a concern for the fish resource. DOF and the state faced continuing litigation, and the tribes had achieved minimal acceptance and minimal gains despite favorable court rulings. The parties at the Fort Ludlow meeting resolved to get through one fishing season going to court as little as possible. A one-year agreement for Puget Sound fisheries aimed to settle disputes between North and South Puget Sound tribes and between sports fishermen and tribes.

It became obvious that managing the fish resource must be taken out of the courts and put into the hands of the state and tribes to sustain the resource. The state and tribes, building on the first-year agreement, took over the Puget Sound Management Plan from the court and renegotiated the plan themselves.

Cooperative management was aggressively expanded under the policies of Governor Booth Gardner, elected in 1984. Tribes and DOF crafted watershed management plans throughout Puget Sound in 1986. Plans for coastal fisheries were negotiated with Olympic Peninsula tribes. As the Northwest Indian Fisheries Commission reports in *Comprehensive Tribal Fisheries Management*, "Cooperative resource management is the basis of natural resource management in the State of Washington. It is a management approach that is unparalleled in the nation. But most importantly, it is a process that helps place the focus of the state and the tribes where it belongs—on the resource."

State leadership that recognized the futility and high cost of a protracted judicial dispute, together with a precipitous decline in fish harvest and a general recognition of the benefits of dispute resolution, as seen in other Washington state conflicts, combined to change the hostile atmosphere to one more amenable to seeking mutually beneficial accommodation.

The Timber-Fish-Wildlife Agreement

The meeting at Port Ludlow in 1986 and the subsequent success of state-tribal fishery management set the stage for negotiating joint, cooperative management of timber, other fisheries, wildlife, and water resources in the state of Washington. The Northwest Resources Center mediated meetings of representatives from tribes, the timber industry, environmental organizations, and state government. They were asked to explore the possibility of agreeing to agree and to develop "win-win" solutions to old problems.

The final timber-fish-wildlife (TFW) agreement in 1987 "provides a process for resolving differences which arise when managing multiple resources. [It is an] agreement of commitment by all parties to work together to reach consensus" for natural resource management concerning forest practices on state and private lands. As the Treaty Indian Tribes of Western Washington note, "TFW is not an institution. It is a living process built on trust, commitment and above all, cooperation." TFW provides for a decision-making process of administrative subcommittees overseeing technical studies, training, information, and education and a policy group to review larger policy questions. Planning, including resource management plans, and annual evaluations contribute to the comprehensive management of resources through TFW.

Other ventures in state-tribal cooperation in Washington state include the Sustainable Forestry Roundtable, the Pacific Salmon Treaty with Canada, and watershed planning. Governor Booth Gardner issued the "Centennial Accord" in 1989, which applauded these agreements and committed the state and tribes to a government-to-government relationship while institutionalizing it throughout state and tribal agencies. Washington's 26 federally recognized Indian tribes joined Governor Booth Gardner in publicly signing the accord in Washington's 100th year of statehood.

Cooperation Protects the Resource

As these case studies illustrate, states and tribes have found that negotiated agreements provide solutions and working relationships that litigation and federal court settlements tend to preclude. Yet court rulings frequently clarify key issues and build the foundation for successful negotiation. Richard Du Bey has suggested that when the legal issues become the focal point and the resource is decimated, nobody wins. Cooperation in resource management directs energy away from litigation and toward protecting the resource for the benefit of Indian and non-Indian users alike.

In sum, negotiations and co-management ventures, in contrast with a destructive adversarial approach that often results from litigation, are more likely to foster constructive interactions. As Elizabeth Checchio and Bonnie Colby conclude, "Beyond the finely worded legal documents, the political maneuvering, and the engineers' blueprints, settlements are based on people building working relationships, people who have expanded their capacity to perceive and appreciate concerns different from their own." Perhaps this approach will make the 1990s the "Decade of Partnerships" as proclaimed by the Native American Fish & Wildlife Society.

References

American Bar Association, National Resources, Energy and Environmental Law Section. *1994: The Year in Review.* Tulsa, Okla.: ABA, 1995.

Cecchio, Elizabeth, and Bonnie G. Colby. *Indian Water Rights: Negotiating the Future.* Tucson, Ariz.: University of Arizona, June, 1993.

The CWAG Reporter (Conference of Western Attorneys General, Sacramento , Calif.). (Fall 1995).

DuBey, Richard A., and Grant D. Parker. "Protection of Reservation Environment— Air and Water Resources Under Federal Law." In *Sovereignty Symposium III: The Dialogue Continues.* Guthrie, Okla.: The Oklahoma Supreme Court, The Oklahoma Indian Affairs Commission, and The Sovereignty Symposium, Inc., 1990.

Getches, David H., Charles F. Wilkinson and Robert Williams. *Federal Indian Law: Cases and Materials.* 3rd. ed. American Casebook Series. St. Paul: West Publishing Co., 1993.

McCool, Daniel. "Command of the Waters: Iron Triangles, Federal Water Development, and Indian Water Rights." *Ecology Law Quarterly* 38 (1987).

Strickland, Rennard, and Maria Proffi. "The Dilemma of Preserving Tribal Culture and Poverty Resource Development." *Natural Resources and Environment* (Spring 1993).

Winters vs. United States, U.S. 456 (1908).

Zelio, Judy A., "Settling Indian Water Rights in Idaho and Wyoming." National Conference of State Legislatures, 1991. Photocopied.

9. ENVIRONMENTAL REGULATION

States and Indian tribes are both dealing with environmental problems of increasing severity and expense. Pollution of the air, the land, or water does not respect state or tribal political boundaries. Pollution control and related problems such as waste disposal and hazardous materials transportation call for a coordinated approach.

In an environmental handbook for tribal leaders, the National Congress of American Indians writes:

> Although not all disputes or problems can or should be resolved through a cooperative approach, environmental protection programs can be especially conducive to coordinated approaches and cooperative efforts by the individual governments. Tribal-state agreements do not and cannot change the jurisdiction of any of the parties. Instead, they accept the jurisdiction framework, and the governments involved agree on mechanisms to coordinate their resources and activities for their common good, just as adjacent states or adjacent counties do. Such agreements often commit the various state, local, and tribal governments to communicating regularly to encourage coordination of their individual efforts, share information, provide technical assistance, and work out arrangements to share facilities or resources.

A key player in state-tribal environmental regulation is the U.S. Environmental Protection Agency (EPA). EPA policy is that tribes should be the primary decision makers on issues of environmental regulation on tribal land. However, tribes often do not have the resources to implement comprehensive environmental programs. A recent survey found that 53 percent of tribes have no environmental protection programs. In such cases, EPA is responsible for environmental regulation in Indian country, and the agency's record of enforcement has been inconsistent. This gap of regulation enforcement on Indian land has raised concerns on the part of state officials for public health and environmental protection on and off the reservation.

States do not have authority to enforce environmental laws on reservations. However, state resources and technical expertise combined with tribal authority to regulate can provide for a negotiated solution. Both governments have concerns for people's health and safety which is affected by activities on and off tribal land. State-tribal cooperation in developing and enforcing coordinated programs for environmental regulation serve the interests of both parties. This chapter examines this type of cooperation in the areas of water quality, waste disposal, and hazardous materials transportation.

Overview of EPA Policy

Federal environmental policy of the early 1970s overlooked the fact that Indian lands were exempt from state authority. EPA delegated to the states the authority to set and enforce standards. Environmental regulatory programs were to be administered by the states according to uniform federal standards for environmental regulation. Federal statutes addressed air and water pollution, hazardous waste disposal, pesticides application, wetlands protection, and surface mining of coal. In the early years of federal environmental programs, EPA focused its energies on fostering relationships with states and funding development of states' regulatory capacity. None of EPA's 27 regulatory programs applied to Indian reservations. The role of tribes in implementing federal programs remained unclear, and the regulatory capacity of tribes remained undeveloped.

EPA adopted a new policy in 1984 that recognized the tribes' authority to develop environmental programs using EPA standards as a minimum. Several principles were outlined to guide EPA's conduct in working with tribes to develop and administer environmental programs affecting reservations. These principles include:

- Working directly with tribes on a government-to-government basis;
- Recognizing tribal authority to set standards, make decisions, and manage reservation programs;
- Considering tribal interests fully in decisions affecting reservations;
- Encouraging cooperation between tribal and state governments;
- Removing legal and procedural impediments to working directly with the tribes;
- Assisting tribes in assuming regulatory and program responsibilities; and
- Enlisting support of other federal agencies on Indian lands.

The trend to include direct reference to Indian tribes in environmental legislation began in the 1980s and continued in the 1990s. Congress amended the Safe Drinking Water Act, the Clean Water Act, the Superfund law, and the Clean Air Act to provide for the treatment of tribes as if they were states. These changes preempt states from regulating environmental quality on reservations. Tribal programs, like state programs, must be consistent with federal legislation.

Tribes are eligible for EPA grants to implement their own regulations within broad EPA standards. For instance, the amended Clean Water Act allows Indian governments to apply for delegated authority to set water quality standards and issue discharge permits. The Isleta Pueblo in New Mexico became the first reservation to receive such authority in October 1992. The pueblo set more stringent requirements than the state of New Mexico, which triggered a lawsuit by the city of Albuquerque. Several more requests for "state" status from tribes quickly followed. Tribes vary in the sufficiency of resources to develop ongoing water quality management programs and meet their wastewater treatment needs. Some are discouraged from applying for programs under the Clean Water Act because of grant eligibility requirements and the multitude of categorical programs.

Federal Jurisdiction and State-Tribal Cooperation

EPA views Indian tribes as the only government unit with jurisdiction over environmental regulations on their lands. EPA works directly with tribal governments and recognizes that they are not political subdivisions of states. Federal agencies enforce environmental regulations when tribes do not have the technical training, funds, or enforcement capability to administer the regulations themselves. EPA retains regulatory jurisdiction over reservations unless a tribe applies for and receives approval to assume primacy within the reservation. Once a tribe is granted primacy, it may take over the administration of laws from EPA to implement national standards. The tribe will then have complete jurisdiction on the reservation. State environmental regulations may be applied to the reservation only if the tribe and the state enter into cooperative agreements in which tribes agree to state

Environmental Health Laboratory of the University of Wisconsin-Superior and the Great Lakes Indian Fish and Wildlife Commission

The Lake Superior Research Institute of the University of Wisconsin-Superior sponsors the Environmental Health Laboratory that works with the 13 tribal governments of the Great Lakes Indian Fish and Wildlife Commission (GLIFWC). The laboratory trains tribal members in environmental science and hopes to make 30 jobs in that field available to tribal members. GLIFWC provides information to the scientific community assessing environmental problems such as water quality and fish toxicity. Because fish is the Indians' predominant food source and important in the tribes' culture, tribal members in the Great Lakes region are a source of information for the scientific community researching water quality.

One area of mutual tribal and state concern is toxicity levels in fish. Some members of the Red Cliff Band of Lake Superior Chippewa Indians (Wisconsin) are being studied to determine the health impacts of ingesting toxics currently found in fish. Shared skills and knowledge will enhance environmental assessment performed by the tribes. Ultimately, the program hopes to advance state and tribal efforts to effectively manage water quality that affects the safety of people on and off reservations.

regulation. Some tribes opt to undertake regulatory responsibility, and others prefer to leave regulation to EPA or to develop a state-tribal partnership.

EPA's delegation of authority to Indian tribes is under challenge in some states. Montana is suing EPA over its granting of authority to administer the Clean Water Act Section 303 to the Confederated Kootenai and Salish Tribes. The tribes' water quality standards would apply to nontribal members owning property within the "checkerboard" reservation. The governor and nontribal landowners argue that the state should have jurisdiction over the land not owned by tribal members. In Wisconsin, state leaders have criticized the expansion of air pollution controls through "redesignation" sought by the Potawatomi tribe. Nearby cities fear that more environmental regulations will threaten the economy.

Nonetheless, the climate for state-tribal cooperation in environmental regulation is generally positive. There are several examples of state-tribal cooperation in environmental regulation:

- Washington and the Puyallup tribe have worked together to manage hazardous wastes under the federal Resource Conservation and Recovery Act (RCRA) implemented on trust and nontrust lands within the reservation.

- The Confederated Tribes of the Colville Reservation and Washington reached an agreement on a procedure for water pollution regulation within reservation boundaries.

- North Dakota and the Fort Berthold reservation agreed to coordinate regulation of pesticide applicators on the reservation.

Many states and tribes share similar environmental concerns, yet their economic and social resources may be vastly different. In the midst of economic disadvantage and unemployment rates averaging 40 percent, tribes are looking for means of economic self-sufficiency that may involve use of Indian land and natural resources. Tribal environmental concerns tend to include protecting fisheries and hunting grounds outside of Indian Country, preventing adverse environmental impacts on reservations from activities off reservations, and maintaining control over air and water quality in Indian Country. States want to avoid adverse environmental impacts on areas around reservations from activities on reservations.

Many tribes do not have the resources to regulate effectively. For instance, most tribes affiliated with the Northwest Indian Fisheries Commission have reported that hiring a water quality expert on tribal staff is a high priority, but they cannot afford to do it. Addressing this concern, several states offer tribes their expertise, testing facilities, and testing programs to evaluate compliance with tribal environmental standards. A few states enhance these programs with training components for tribal members interested in environmental management and regulation.

Waste Disposal on Indian Land

Reservations are among the last large tracts of nonpublic, largely undeveloped land. Furthermore, most Indian land is not subject to state regulations governing solid and hazardous waste, and federal laws are less stringent than those of certain states. Between 1990 and 1993, as many landfills shut down because of stricter federal standards, the waste industry examined Indian lands as potential sites for new landfills, as well as for facilities for hazardous and radioactive waste management and disposal. By one count, waste companies made offers to more than 50 Indian tribes for landfills and hazardous waste incinerators in 1990 through 1992. At the same time, the U.S. Department of Energy sought volunteers to store spent nuclear fuel, most of which were Indian tribes. An ongoing test of state-tribal relations is the Mescalero Apache Tribe's effort to develop a spent fuel storage facility on its land in New Mexico.

Tribes have exercised their sovereignty to decide whether commercial waste projects serve their best interests. Some have decided to exclude certain land uses and refused the companies' offers. Other tribes accepted the proposals for the capital and jobs they bring to the reservations to offset unemployment and economic depression, sometimes over the objections of tribal members who cite traditional beliefs in the sacredness of the land as well as distrust of project sponsors' safety claims. State regulators, interested in ensuring that tribal waste sites meet the same level of safety as those regulated by the state, but finding that they have no jurisdiction, are turning to intergovernmental agreements to create interjurisdictional bridges for environmental management of waste facilities.

Although tribes cannot be forced by state or local governments to accept or reject dumps on Indian land, a 1989 Supreme Court ruling confused the issue of tribal jurisdiction on reservations. *Brendale vs. Confederated Tribes and Bands of the Yakima Indian Council* involved a zoning dispute between tribes and two non-Indian developers who wanted to use tribal land in a way prohibited by the tribal zoning code but permitted by the county. The Supreme Court ruled that the tribes did not have the right to zone land owned by non-Indians in a part of the reservation owned mostly by non-Indians, but they did in the area owned 97 percent by the tribes. The zoning authority for the land in question thus was granted to Yakima County.

The case holds implications for tribal jurisdiction on non-Indian reservation lands. David Getches, professor of law at the University of Colorado, believes the ruling created tremendous uncertainty about whether tribal or state jurisdiction applies on non-Indian lands. For instance, a non-Indian landowner wishing to develop land as a landfill could possibly resist the extension of tribal land use restrictions. Mervyn Tano of the Council of Energy Resource Tribes believes that the ruling requires tribes, in effect, to prove that their environmental regulations are necessary to protect residents' health and welfare. It will be harder to claim jurisdiction if there is no direct effect on Indian residents. Thus, it remains unclear who has environmental jurisdiction over activities on non-Indian landholdings within reservations. The ruling provides an incentive for states, counties, and tribes to work together to negotiate jurisdictional agreements and to develop a comprehensive approach to environmental management and regulation. This approach may also help with the problem of cleaning up an estimated 600 open waste dumps on Indian lands, which pose a greater environmental threat than new facilities.

The California-Campo Band Compromise

In 1989, the Campo Band of Kumeyaay Indians was approached to create a landfill on 660 acres of tribal land 60 miles east of San Diego. Neighboring ranchers and farmers protested the idea and complained that the tribe was ignoring environmental concerns. People opposed to the dump feared toxic contamination of the air and groundwater from a landfill unregulated by the state. In response to those fears, and concerned with potentially weak federal enforcement of environmental regulations, California Assemblyman Steve Peace introduced a bill in February 1990 to prohibit hazardous waste disposal on Indian lands unless all applicable federal, state, and local regulations were met. The bill failed and was reintroduced in 1991 to include the regulation of solid waste facilities and transportation of solid wastes. Indian tribes opposed both versions of the Peace bill as an affront to tribal sovereignty. In the meantime, nine other proposals to site waste facilities in California were announced.

The Campo Band asserted that the waste disposal facility would be the most fruitful of the few options available for economic development. The band formed the Campo Environmental Protection Agency in 1990 to enforce environmental standards and to oversee the development of the disposal facility, as well as a hazardous waste recycling facility on land belonging to another Indian group, the La Posta Band of Mission Indians. The tribe developed environmental regulations and expertise while asserting its freedom from state regulation. Through its power to approve the landfill, the federal Bureau of Indian Affairs took the lead in preparing an environmental impact statement (EIS). A federal district court judge found the EIS adequate under the National Environmental Policy Act in a 1994 ruling.

The state was concerned with the potential political and environmental consequences of state failure to regulate the disposal site. Peace drafted a new bill in June 1991 that incorporated a structure for tribes and the state to enter into voluntary agreements for joint regulation of proposed waste facilities. After a series of harsh legislative battles, Peace's amended bill passed both houses that summer, and Governor Pete Wilson signed the bill into law in October 1991. The band and the state agreed to negotiate, litigation was avoided, and an agreement was reached. The resulting legislation embodies compromise.

Under the legislation, responsibility for environmental regulation was allocated in a way both parties could tolerate. Each side compromised to reach the agreement while retaining a certain number of conflicting claims. The Campo Band asserted that only tribal and federal regulations were applicable on the reservation but agreed to prepare environmental impact statements and to adopt state law as the minimum standard. The state agreed to furnish technical assistance but did not concede its argument that it had jurisdiction over the site. Tribal parties acknowledged the state's legitimate environmental concerns and more sophisticated regulatory structure, while the state recognized the tribes' valid right to govern their own lands and eased its stance of criminalizing facilities without permits.

The California legislation mandates that the state share regulatory power in cases where an agreement can be reached and creates a structure allowing joint exercise of jurisdiction using a government-to-government relationship. Parties to a voluntary agreement must meet the guidelines outlined in the bill. Provisions in an agreement must be functionally equivalent to those contained in state law. Requirements for information-sharing, dispute

---

Cherokee-North Carolina Agreement for Emergency Planning

The Eastern Band of the Cherokee and the Emergency Response Commission of the state of North Carolina signed a memorandum of understanding on July 9, 1989, stating that the two parties recognize each other's authority. The principal chief of the Eastern Band of the Cherokee Indians nominates people to serve on the local emergency planning committee, and both the North Carolina Emergency Response Commission and the Cherokees' local emergency planning commission perform duties relating to emergency planning.

The agreement between the Cherokees and North Carolina preserves the sovereignty of both entities. Moreover, by agreeing to treat the area as a local emergency planning district and by setting out the duties of both parties, the Eastern Band of the Cherokee and the North Carolina Emergency Response Commission have enhanced emergency preparedness in the area. The agreement was made possible by the new federal interpretation of the Emergency Planning and Community Right-to-Know Act (Title III of the Superfund Amendments and Reauthorization Act of 1986), which authorizes Indian tribes to implement hazardous materials emergency planning similar to that performed by state and local governments.

---

resolution, access to sites, and review of documents are clearly defined. Either party can sue the other for breach of the agreement. The state retains ultimate enforcement power under any such agreement if there is an imminent threat to public health, safety, or the environment and the tribe fails to act—a concession to environmental interest groups in the state. A tribe's right to respond is protected with strict requirements for notification before the state takes any enforcement action.

The Campo EPA and California EPA struck an agreement under the new law in 1992, which provided the basis for a cooperative regulatory effort. The landfill moved another step closer to construction with the issuance of a final air quality permit by the U.S. EPA in August 1995.

Hazardous Materials Transportation

An emerging area for state-tribal cooperation is hazardous materials transportation. State and local governments have sought control over the transportation of hazardous and nuclear materials, including waste, for the past decade. (Under federal law nuclear materials are a subset of hazardous materials, while in many states separate laws govern nuclear materials and hazardous materials.) The Hazardous Materials Transportation Uniform Safety Act (HMTUSA) (P.L. 101-615), passed by Congress in October 1990, clearly defines state authority in relation to the federal government in routing designations, enforcement of similar laws, and assessment of fees.

In several regions of the country, Indian tribal governments also are examining their authority over the movement of hazardous and nuclear materials through their land. Interstate highways, the preferred route for such materials, run through or near at least 80 Indian reservations in 17 states. The new hazardous materials law authorizes tribes to exercise greater power over hazardous materials transportation in their jurisdictions. However, jurisdictional overlap creates uncertainty regarding the regulation of the transportation of such materials. Some resolution of jurisdictional questions will become necessary as more nuclear materials, such as high-level waste, transuranic waste, and spent fuel are transported on the nation's highways and rail lines.

Passage of the HMTUSA opens further possibilities for state-tribal cooperation. HMTUSA explicitly recognizes Indian tribes in most places where state and local governments are mentioned. This recognition gives tribes new authority to designate routes for all hazardous material transportation (using federal standards), to enforce requirements that are "substantively the same as" federal provisions, to assess "equitable" fees for hazardous materials transportation, and to receive federal grants for training public employees in emergency response procedures. It also places tribes under the preemptive provisions of federal hazardous materials transportation regulation.

Developing emergency preparedness for hazardous materials accidents presents opportunities for better integration of state and tribal resources. Tribes, like states, need funding to support an emergency response infrastructure. In general, they need training, personnel, equipment, and planning assistance, but they are not receiving it in adequate amounts from states or the federal government. Grants under HMTUSA help but are small.

The Council of Energy Resource Tribes recently found that state and local governments are developing response capabilities for hazardous materials emergencies with substantial federal assistance, but such "emergency preparedness in the overwhelming majority of Indian tribes is seriously deficient or virtually non-existent." A survey conducted by the Transportation Research Center at Indiana University for the U.S. Nuclear Regulatory Commission substantiated this when it concluded that tribal preparedness to manage transportation accidents involving hazardous materials is linked to the broader issue of tribal sovereignty and full tribal participation in a variety of regulatory areas. In other words, most tribes have not yet developed the governmental capacity to address emergency preparedness. Only a few of the tribes surveyed were prepared to conduct emergency response training, including the Gila River Indian Community, the Pueblo of Acoma, and the Confederated Tribes of the Umatilla Indian Reservation, but most indicated their intention to assume first response responsibility on tribal lands. Many also would like to establish memoranda of understanding with adjacent states for technical assistance. However, jurisdictional disputes and the intransigence of some states in recognizing tribal sovereignty hamper efforts to establish emergency response agreements, according to this survey.

Tribal and state governments have, nonetheless, forged cooperative agreements concerning hazardous materials. Oregon law requires consultation with officials of the Confederated Tribes of the Umatilla Indian Reservation on transportation matters under the Pacific States Radioactive Materials Transportation Committee. The Idaho Department of Transportation and the Shoshone Bannock Tribes have an agreement covering traffic enforcement, which includes radioactive materials transportation. A 1989 study by NCSL found general transportation agreements between at least 16 states and adjacent Indian tribes.

States and tribes do find that they can exercise mutually beneficial joint jurisdiction. In areas where transportation is minimal and where they feel their interests are adequately protected, tribes may prefer to leave regulation of hazardous materials transportation up to the state. On reservations where hazardous materials transportation is heavy, however, tribes may enact reasonable regulation like the Shoshone-Bannock tribes have done without diminishing state sovereignty, as long as it is consistent with similar federal regulation. All parties would benefit if training in first response measures, similar to that which state and local authorities receive, were available to appropriate tribal authorities. Tribes may wish to enact registration requirements with fees for carriers to help cover the costs of such training. More burdensome regulations may prove less useful to tribes since they may shift the focus onto legal issues, away from the potential dangers of hazardous materials transportation. For example, the Prairie Island Mdewakanton Sioux Indian Community's ordinance on radioactive materials transportation was found to be preempted in 1992 because it was inconsistent with the federal Hazardous Materials Transportation Act. As states and tribes work with the federal government in the implementation of HMTUSA, they may discover more areas for cooperation.

Conclusion

States and tribes have different priorities in land use and environmental regulation that are complicated by questions of jurisdiction. Tribes have the authority to set up their own environmental programs using EPA standards as a minimum, yet they often lack the resources for comprehensive oversight and enforcement. Several states do offer technical assistance and train tribal members in environmental assessment and regulation enforcement to the benefit of both parties. Ultimately, coordinating regulation efforts is an effective means for the administration of environmental law. Cooperative working relationships clearly strengthen the ability of both states and tribes to comprehensively address environmental problems. As former Idaho Attorney General Larry EchoHawk says: "As we confront the complex issues of the 1990s, let's stop and remember the circling hawks, that towering mountain, that incredible salmon. We seek to find the elusive balance between our pocketbooks and our spirits. Let's be wise stewards of this land."

References

Ambler, Marjane. "On the Reservations: No Haste, No Waste." *Planning* (November 1991): 26-29.

Beasley, Conger Jr. "Dances with Garbage." *E Magazine* (November/December 1991): 38-41.

Commission on State-Tribal Relations. *Handbook on State-Tribal Relations.* Albuquerque: American Indian Law Center, Inc., 1983.

Connolly, Michael. "Intergovernmental Cooperation: A Case Study on the Campo EPA—An Ancient Role in a Modern Context." *Environmental Law* 14, no. 2: (Spring/Summer 1995).

Council of Energy Resource Tribes. *Development of Hazardous Materials Transportation Safety Programs by Indian Tribal Governments. Part 1 of Background, Government Roles, and Options for Program Planning.* Denver: CERT, 1989.

EchoHawk, Larry. "The White Man Turned A Tame, Beautiful Land Into the Wild West." *High Country News*, May 9, 1992.

"EPA Proposal on Treatment of Indian Tribes as States under Section 404 of the Clean Water Act." 54 *Federal Register 149180*, November 29, 1989.

Foster, Barbara, and James B. Reed. "State-Tribal Transportation Agreements." *State Legislative Report*, 14, no. 4 (1989).

Frey, Bertram C., "Legal Opinion Regarding Delegation of Partial RCRA Program to Menominee Indian Tribe of Wisconsin." U.S. EPA, Region 5, Chicago, November 3, 1989. Memorandum to Valdas V. Adamkus.

Getches, David H. "Intergovernmental Agreements with Indian Tribes in the United States: Some Lessons for Canada?" Paper read at Canadian Bar Association Program on Constitutional Entrenchment of Aboriginal Self-Government, March 27, 1992, at Ottawa, Ontario, Canada.

"Hazardous Materials Transportation Act of 1990." Public Law 101-615. November 16, 1990.

"Indians Volunteer Reservation for Big Dump, Set off Uprising." *Denver Post*, January 21, 1990.

"State Plans Suit to Reverse Key EPA Tribal Water Jurisdictional Call." *Inside EPA*. March 10, 1995.

"Memorandum of Understanding." Agreement Between the Eastern Band of the Cherokee and the Emergency Response Commission of the State of North Carolina, July 9, 1989.

National Congress of American Indians. *Environmental Protection in Indian Country: A Handbook for Tribal Leaders and Resource Managers.* Washington, D.C., N.D.

New Mexico Office of Indian Affairs. Memorandum to Governor Bruce King on state/tribal issues, May 6, 1991.

Reed, James B. "Interactions Between States and Tribes." Paper presented at National Congress of American Indians and U.S. Department of Energy Tribal Seminar on Nuclear Waste, Phoenix, Ariz., September 12, 1989.

Reed, James B., and Judy Zelio. "The Compromise Continues. . ." *State Legislatures* (March 1992): 12-17.

Ruckelshaus, William D. "EPA Policy for the Administration of Environmental Programs on Indian Reservations," United States Environmental Protection Agency Indian Policy. Washington, D.C.: EPA, 1989.

Tousley, Dean. "Tribal Regulation of Transportation." Paper presented at National Congress of American Indians and U.S. Department of Energy Tribal Seminar on Nuclear Waste, Phoenix, Ariz., September 1989.

The Treaty Indian Tribes in Washington State. *Model Tribal Water Quality Program.* Olympia, Wash.: The Northwest Indian Fisheries Commission, n.d.

U.S. Congress, Senate Special Committee on Investigations of the Select Committee on Indian Affairs. *Final Report and Legislative Recommendations.* 101st Cong., 1st sess., November 20, 1989.

"U.S. EPA Pilot Project, Menominee Indian Reservation, Wisconsin." November 3, 1989. Photocopied.

Vilardo, Frank J.; Eric L. Mitter; James A. Palmer; Henry C. Briggs; and Julie Fesenmaier. *Survey of State and Tribal Emergency Response Capabilities for Radiological Transportation Incidents.* Prepared for the U.S. Nuclear Regulatory Commission. Bloomington, Ind.: Transportation Research Center, School of Public and Environmental Affairs, Indiana University, 1990.

Western Governors' Association. "Western State-Tribal Relations." Draft. February 29, 1988.

Wilkinson, Charles F. *American Indians, Time and the Law.* New Haven: Yale University Press, 1987.

"Will Waste Be Dumped on Indians?" *Denver Post.* July 29, 1991.

Wolfley, Jeannette. "Tribal Regulatory Nuclear Waste Activities in Indian Country." Paper presented at Fifth Annual International Conference on High Level Radioactive Waste Management. Las Vegas, Nev., May 22-26, 1994.

Zelio, Judy A., ed. "Promoting Effective State-Tribal Relations: A Dialogue." Denver: National Conference of State Legislatures, 1989.

10. SOLUTIONS FOR THE 21ST CENTURY

Closer working relationships between states and Indian tribes have many benefits, as outlined in the preceding chapters. To seek such relationships and to make them work requires governmental leaders to take a fresh look at problem-solving. The thoughtful people whose works are cited throughout this summary, as well as many others, can provide valuable perspectives and advice, but the day-to-day efforts of state and tribal officials are needed to craft creative state-tribal governmental relationships within the American federal system.

The intergovernmental role of tribal governments is dynamic; it causes continual assessment of federal law and policies, case law, and the role of the states under the Constitution, as well as frequent evaluation of the effects of state policies on citizens who can be exempt from those policies. In this sense, Indian tribes make a tremendous contribution to the strength of American government by keeping state attorneys general on the alert, calling upon Congress to make good its promises, and reminding us all that a "great nation keeps it word."

The review by NCSL's Task Force on State-Tribal Relations of the current condition of state-tribal relations has resulted in the findings and recommendations that follow. The findings and recommendations are not new—they are rooted in the work of those who have given these matters a great deal of thought and in the experiences of those who have given practical application to the ideas. It is not the policy of NCSL to advise state legislatures on courses of action; therefore, the recommendations should be viewed only as suggestions for consideration by policymakers.

Findings

1. Indian tribes are legitimate governmental entities within the U.S. federal system.

2. The federal government, while continuing to protect tribal interests, is encouraging tribal governments to assume ever-greater responsibilities. Those responsibilities place heavier financial demands on tribal governments and more management responsibilities on tribal officials.

3. Interactions between state governments and tribal governments have increased significantly in the past 20 years.

4. State governments possess defined constitutional powers that sometimes overlap areas defined by Indian tribes as being also within tribal jurisdiction.

5. Jurisdictional uncertainties and economic competition between Indian and non-Indian interests prompt most state-tribal disputes.

6. A government-to-government relationship is the appropriate starting point for tribes and states to seek resolution of their jurisdictional differences.

7. In a government-to-government relationship, both a state and a tribe recognize the right of the other entity to protect the health, safety, and welfare of its citizens.

8. In a government-to-government relationship, officials of equal governmental stature and with similar governmental authority deal with each other on matters of mutual concern.

9. Intergovernmental agreements are a key mechanism for promoting effective state-tribal relationships.

10. The federal government already requires the negotiation of state-tribal agreements in child welfare and casino gambling.

11. Face-to-face negotiations are preferable to litigation of state-tribal disputes, in many cases. Such negotiations can increase understanding of the needs of the parties as well as outline the constraints on what can and cannot be accomplished by such an approach.

12. State recognition of tribal sovereignty is symbolically very important to tribal members.

13. State recognition of tribal sovereignty can be accomplished within the context of negotiated intergovernmental agreements.

14. Many examples of effective state-tribal agreements can be seen in such areas as law enforcement, transportation, child welfare, taxation, gambling, health care, environmental regulation, and education.

15. Greater efforts to acknowledge the history, contributions, and current role of Indian tribes and Indian people to the United States are needed. State legislatures can take the lead in such efforts.

16. Greater effort on the part of tribes is needed to understand state governments and how they work.

Suggestions

To the President:

A position in the executive intergovernmental affairs office should be specifically designated to deal exclusively with tribes.

To Congress:

1. Congress should enact legislation to encourage states and tribes to enter into intergovernmental agreements for their mutual benefit.

2. Congress should establish and fund a national mediation board to settle state-tribal disputes that the parties are unable to resolve on their own, before litigation and at the request of both disputing parties.

3. Congress should reorganize the Bureau of Indian Affairs to make it more efficient and more responsive to the needs of tribal governments.

4. Congress should determine and implement ways to better coordinate the delivery of federal programs for Native Americans than the BIA.

5. Congress should give high priority to funding the efforts contained in agreements reached by states and tribes through negotiation.

To States:

1. States should carefully consider the merits of negotiated settlements before undertaking litigation to resolve state-tribal jurisdictional disputes.

2. State legislatures should work with tribes to pass legislation outlining a process by which negotiations with Indian tribes can be conducted.

3. States should pass legislation allowing state agencies and political subdivisions to enter into intergovernmental agreements with Indian tribes.

4. States should establish an interagency council to coordinate the activities of state government relative to state-tribal relations.

5. States with ongoing policy questions related to Indian tribes in the state should take steps to establish a legislative Indian affairs committee.

6. State leaders should maintain relationships with tribal leaders on a variety of issues, not just the crises.

7. States should establish educational programs for state employees to expand their knowledge of tribal governments and Indian perspectives.

To Tribes:

1. Tribes should carefully consider the merits of negotiated settlements before undertaking litigation to resolve state-tribal jurisdictional disputes.

2. Tribal leaders should recognize that state governmental policies can have significant effects on tribal members, both negative and positive.

3. Tribal leaders should recognize that state policies and state laws, for the most part, are created by the state legislatures.

4. Tribes should endeavor to work with state leaders in establishing a government-to-government relationship.

5. Tribal leaders should maintain relationships with state leaders on a variety of issues, not just the crises.

6. Tribes should encourage education of tribal members about the structure of state government and its impact on tribes.

Other Recommendations:

In recent reports, the Michigan Law Revision Commission and the Montana Legislative Committee on Indian Affairs offer recommendations and advice that may benefit other states. In its 1993 report, the Michigan commission identified nine areas where further legislation or reform may be appropriate:

1. Developing a procedure for mutual recognition of judgments and orders between Michigan state and tribal courts.

2. Studying and proposing legislation relative to the extradition of persons from tribes to states.

3. Adopting an official state policy regarding government-to-government relations with Native American tribes.

4. Adopting more extensive protection of archeological sites and repatriation of human remains and funerary objects.

5.   Repealing the Michigan limitation on delivery of alcohol to reservations, which is likely unconstitutional.

6.   Studying and reforming the Michigan Indian Affairs Commission.

7.   Exploring changes to Michigan probate law to recognize tribal laws and customs regarding inheritance of property.

8.   If warranted, adopting legislation to protect Indian arts and crafts from fraudulent practices.

9.   Exploring taxation issues relative to tribes and tribal members.

The March 1995 handbook for Montana legislators, *The Tribal Nations of Montana,* lists seven basic principles of state-tribal relations that serve as a fitting conclusion to this book and an excellent basis for 21st century solutions to state-tribal problems.

Indians are not just members of an ethnic minority group in Montana.   Most Indians are also members of distinct cultural nations with a special political and legal status that has been enshrined in the U.S. Constitution, bolstered by subsequent federal laws, and affirmed by the courts.

Tribal governments are not subordinate to state governments and are not bound by state laws.   With rare exceptions, a state has jurisdiction within a reservation only to the extent that Congress has delegated specific authority to it or in situations in which neither federal nor tribal law preempt state law.

There is always a federal dimension to consider in formal state-tribal interactions.   Tribal governments are subordinate to Congress.   In many areas of governance, including economic development, environmental regulation, and law enforcement, tribal authorities require authorization, appropriations, and approval from the secretary of the interior or lower-ranking officials of the Interior Department's Bureau of Indian Affairs (BIA).

Federal Indian policy is generally consistent in some aspects and remarkably inconsistent in others.   The separation of powers allows the coexistence of contrasting views and con-tradictory decisions: Every U.S. President since President Nixon has espoused self-determination as a guiding principle.   Congress has both broadly encouraged self-government and in some instances prescribed in detail the manner in which tribes may use their self-governing authority.   Federal and U.S. Supreme Court decisions have see-sawed between supporting and limiting the sovereignty of Indian nations.

The Indian nations of Montana are similar in some general respects but distinct from each other in many important ways.   Although "Indian Country" is a useful phrase when considering federal laws and policies applicable to all Indian nations, each nation is unique, with different priorities, values, cultural attributes, and economic circumstances.   The distinctions between different Indian nations in Montana need to be considered in discussions and negotiations between the state government and tribal governments.

Government-to-government relations are the norm, not the exception.   Protocol is important.   The use of proper channels demonstrates mutual respect and lends dignity to relationships that are often delicate and easily tainted by misunderstanding and the suspicion that state (or federal) bureaucrats are attempting to interfere with internal disputes of tribal government officials.

The leaders and other members of Indian nations are generally wary of state government. Western American history is peppered with examples of coercion, massacres, broken treaties, disingenuous overtures of peace and friendship, disrespect, and attempts to assert rights and usurp powers in contravention of federal law and policy.

As Bradford Keeney has noted: "The time has come for us to appreciate, value, and honor our differences." Let us begin a new century.

References

Keeney, Bradford. *Shaking Out the Spirits.* (Barrytown, N.Y.: Station Hill Press, 1994): 161.

Michigan Law Revision Commission. "Study Report: Michigan's Legislative Power Over Its Native American Population." In *28th Annual Report 1993.* Ann Arbor, Mich.: West Publishing Co., 1993.

Montana Legislative Committee on Legislative Affairs. *The Tribal Nations of Montana: A Handbook for Legislators.* Helena, Mont.: Montana Legislative Council, March 1995.

**Members of the Task Force on State-Tribal Relations
National Conference of State Legislatures
1990-1993**

Penobscot Representative Priscilla Attean, Maine
Representative John Cashman, Maine
Senator Sam Cassidy, Colorado
Senator James Dunn, South Dakota
Representative Larry Gabriel, South Dakota
Senator Delwyn Gage, Montana
Representative Emil Grieser, Oklahoma
Representative Richard Hagen, South Dakota
Senator Enoch Kelly Haney, Oklahoma
Senator Ben Hanley, Arizona
Representative William Harbor, Iowa
Representative Allen Hightower, Texas
Representative Dominic Jacobetti, Michigan
Senator Robert Jauch, Wisconsin
Senator Terry Jordan, Mississippi
Senator Georgianna Lincoln, Alaska
Representative John Medinger, Wisconsin
Senator Jack Metcalf, Washington
Representative Lynda Morgan, New Mexico
Senator John Pinto, New Mexico
Senator Robert Presley, California
Representative Scott Ratliff, Wyoming
Assemblyman Steven Sanders, New York
Representative Albert Shirley, New Mexico
Representative John Solbach, Kansas
Representative Jane Svoboda, Iowa
Senator William Truban, Virginia
Senator Leonard Tsosie, New Mexico

In November 1993, the issue of state-tribal relations was added to the jurisdiction of the State-Local Committee, which was renamed the State, Local and Tribal Relations Committee of the Assembly on the Legislature. In July 1994, the Fiscal, Oversight and Intergovernmental Affairs Committee of the Assembly on State Issues assumed responsibility for state-tribal relations.

APPENDIX B

**Meetings of the Task Force on State-Tribal Relations
National Conference of State Legislatures
1990-1993**

Location and Date	Speakers	Topics
Boise, Idaho April 1, 1990	P. Sam DeLoria Joseph DeLaCruz Larry EchoHawk Michelle Aguilar Michael Nugent Marvin Osborne	◆ Review State-Tribal Commission ◆ Set goals for task force
Nashville, Tennessee August 6-8, 1990	Browning Pipestem Patricia Zell Representative Priscilla Attean Senator William Truban Senator Bob Jauch Linda Lewis Allen Slickpoo Roger Novotny	◆ Sovereignty ◆ Federal Legislation ◆ State-tribal relations ◆ Survey of states and tribes requested ◆ Tax agreements
Washington, D.C. December 12, 1990	Mary McClure Wayne Ducheneaux Gay Kingman Richard Trudell David Harrison LaDonna Harris Kimberly Craven Tim Wapato Bill Lovell Indian Gaming Commissioner Anthony Hope Joel Starr Dwight McKay Richard Keister Tassie Hanna Dan Lewis	◆ Government-to-government relations ◆ Common ground

Lincoln, Nebraska
April 12, 1991
	Indian Gaming Commissioner
	  Anthony Hope
	Navajo Nation Vice President
	  Don LaPointe
	Tom Witty
	Robert Peregoy
		◆ Gaming and economic development
		◆ Reburial and repatriation

Orlando, Florida August 11, 1991	Senator Joseph Mazurek Navajo Nation Vice President Marshall Plummer Michael Jackson	◆ State-tribal agreements

Location and Date	Speakers	Topics
Washington, D.C. October 21, 1991	Congressman Ben Campbell Senator E. Kelly Haney Representative Larry Gabriel Representative Scott Ratliff Derrick Watchman Harley Duncan Craig Sweeney Douglas Endreson Manley Begay William Stringer Joseph Membrino Representative Robert Johnson Wisconsin Attorney General James Doyle	◆ Taxes and state-tribal tax agreements
Portland, Maine September 28, 1991	Tribal Governor James Sappier Tom Tureen Mary Philbrook	◆ Quincentennial ◆ Passamaquaddy economic development ◆ Arts
Kansas City, Missouri May 28, 1992	Michael Cox Senator Charles Berg Kansas Deputy Attorney General Julene Miller Mervyn Tano David Leroy Susan Smith Julie Jordan Representative Bob Light	◆ Tribal gaming ◆ Nuclear waste storage and disposal ◆ Transportation
Cincinnati, Ohio July 28, 1992	Tribal Chairman gaiashkibos Eddye McClure	◆ "The Next 500 Years"
Phoenix, Arizona April 3, 1993	Tony Machukay Tribal Chairman Clinton Pattea	◆ Economic development ◆ Tribal casino tour ◆ Review draft final report
San Diego, California July 26, 1993	Representative Priscilla Attean Kevin Gover Richard Hill Tim Wapato	◆ Tribal sovereignty ◆ Solid waste disposal ◆ Tribal gaming
Phoenix, Arizona October 21, 1993	Representative Ben Hanley Alph Secakuku Gloria Lomahaftewa Sherry Hutt Cecil Antone Lillian Seibel Senator Paul Valandra	◆ Indian artists ◆ Labor issues ◆ Artifacts and sacred objects ◆ Approval of final report

INDEX

I

ICWA. *See* Indian Child Welfare Act
Idaho, gaming in, 40, 41, 42; hazardous materials
    transportation in, 69; hunting/fishing/wildlife accords in,
    12, 18; tax issues in, 47, 48; water rights in, 12, 17, 56-
    57
IGRA. *See* Indian Gaming Regulatory Act
IHB. *See* Indian Health Board
IHS. *See* Indian Health Service
Illinois, gaming in, 40
Income taxes, 46-47
Indian Affairs Commission (Alabama), 8
Indian Affairs Commission (Michigan), reforming, 74
Indian Affairs Commission (South Dakota), 41
Indian Child Welfare Act (ICWA) (1978), 28-29
Indian Country, 4, 5, 36, 75
Indian Gaming Regulatory Act (IGRA) (1988), problems
    with, 42, 44; states and, 39-44
Indian Health Board (IHB) (Minnesota), 23
Indian Health Service (IHS), 21, 35
Indian Nations at Risk, 27
Indian Reorganization Act (1934), 16
Indian Student Bill of Rights, adoption of, 27
Integrated Waste Management Board (California),
    sovereignty and, 10
Intergovernmental agreements, 12, 17-18, 73
Interior Committee (U.S. House), gaming issues and, 42
Internal Revenue Service, employment taxes/tribes and, 46
Iowa, gaming in, 40, 41

J

Joint Committee on Gaming Compacts (Kansas), gaming
    and, 41
Joint Committee on State-Tribal Relations (Oklahoma),
    gaming and, 41
Joint Powers Agreement Act (1978), child welfare and, 29
Jurisdiction, 10; conflicts over, 13, 15, 16; federal, 64-66;
    state-tribal, 5-6

K

Kansas, gaming in, 40, 41; tax issues in, 48
Kansas ex rel. Stephan vs. Finney, 41
Keeney, Bradford: quote of, 76
Kickapoos, sales tax and, 47
Kumeyaays, waste disposal facility and, 67-68

L

Lakota Fund, 32-33
Land claims, 3, 11, 13, 18
Land use, contention over, 36; priorities in, 70
Laurence, Robert: on sovereignty, 5
Law Revision Commission (Michigan), recommendations
    by, 74

Legislative Committee on Indian Affairs (Montana),
    recommendations by, 74
Legislative Coordinating Council (Kansas), gaming and, 41
Legislative Council (North Dakota), gaming and, 42
Legislative Indian Affairs Committee, 8
Lester, David: on state-tribal relations, 1; on tribal
    economies, 35
Liquor taxes, 51
Litigation, 15, 18-19, 50, 73, 74; fishing rights, 59; gaming,
    43; natural resource, 54; taxation, 52; water rights, 57
Louisiana, gaming in, 9, 40, 41, 42; tax issues in, 51

M

McCarran Amendment (1952), water rights and, 55
McCool, Daniel: water rights and, 55
McCoy, Melody: on education, 25
Maine, hunting/fishing/wildlife accords in, 12; land claims
    issues in, 11; Native American population of, 2; revenue
    sharing in, 12; tax issues in, 48
Marshall, John: on tribes, 5
Maryland, reburial in, 12
Massachusetts, gaming in, 40
Medicaid/Medicare, patient revenues from, 23
Medicine, Bea: *washichu* and, 15
Menominees, loan program of, 33
Mescalero Apaches, spent fuel storage facilities and, 66;
    tourism and, 34
Michael, Joel: state-tribal tax issues and, 51
Michigan, foster care/child protection in, 11; gaming in, 9,
    40; health care in, 22; hunting/fishing/wildlife accords in,
    12; judgements/orders in, 74; \probate law in, 75;
    transportation issues in, 12
Micro-enterprises, 32, 33
Mining/minerals, 8, 35
Minnesota, economic development in, 33, 34; education
    in, 12, 24, 27; gaming in, 40, 41; health care in, 23;
    housing in, 12; hunting/fishing/wildlife accords in, 12,
    58; intergovernmental agreements in, 12; sovereignty
    issues in, 9; tax issues in, 48, 51; tribal relations in, 12
Mission Indians, 67
Mission schools, 26
Mississippi, gaming in, 40; tax issues in, 47, 49
Missouri, gaming in, 40
Montana, arts and crafts protection in, 34; child welfare in,
    11, 30; education in, 25, 26, 27; gaming in, 40, 41;
    hunting/fishing/wildlife accords in, 12; judgements/orders
    in, 74; jurisdiction problems in, 16; legal status in, 75;
    Native American population of, 2; natural resources
    protection in, 34; tax issues in, 48, 49, 51; water rights
    in, 12, 17
Montana University System, 25
Mortality rates, 23

N

National Association of Attorneys General, IGRA and, 42

Resource Conservation and Recovery Act (RCRA),
    hazardous wastes and, 65
Resource management. *See* Natural resources
Rhode Island, gaming in, 40
Rights of Indians and Tribes, The (Pevar), 45
Rights-of-way, negotiating, 35
Rosebud Sioux, education code of, 25; tax compact with,
    52
Rumsey Indian Rancheria vs. Governor Pete Wilson (1994),
    43
Rural Indian Health Board (California), 22

S

Sacred lands, 4, 8
Safe Drinking Water Act, 64
Sales taxes, 47
Salish Kootenai College, 27
Salmon fisheries, 36; state-tribal management of, 58-59
Salt River Pima-Maricopas, water rights and, 17
Santa Clara Pueblo, tax compact with, 51
Scholarships/grants, 24
Schools, Native American, 26-28
Select Committee on Children, Youth and Families (U.S.
    House of Representatives), alcohol/Native Americans
    and, 21
Self-determination, 2, 19, 32; gaming and, 42; taxation and,
    52
Self-Determination/Self-Governance Act, 35
Self-government, 2, 3; gaming and, 42
Seminoles, tobacco taxes and, 49; water rights and, 17
Seminole Tribe of Florida vs. State of Florida (1995), 43
Seneca Nation, taxation and, 48
Severance taxes, 48
Shoshone, self-governance by, 3
Shoshone-Bannock, hazardous materials and, 69; water
    rights and, 17, 56, 57
Sinte Gleska College, 27
Snake River Basin, water rights in, 56, 57
Social Security (FICA), 46, 47
South Dakota, arts and crafts protection in, 34; child
    welfare in, 11, 30; education in, 25, 26, 27; gaming in,
    40, 41, 43; Native American population of, 2; tax issues
    in, 11, 48, 52; tourism in, 34
Sovereignty, 3, 4, 8, 18; limits on, 5, 9; recognition/exercise
    of, 9-10, 73; state-tribal relations and, 12, 13
Spokane Tribe vs. Washington, 43
Standing Rock Sioux, tax compact with, 52
State government, cooperation with, 19; mistrust of, 76;
    native hiring in, 8; state-tribal relations and, 18, 74; tribal
    governments and, 75
State taxes, 47-48
Stevens Treaties (1854, 1855), 58-59
State-Tribal Agreements: A Comprehensive Study, 15
State-tribal relations, federal dimension of, 75; improving,
    v-vi, 6, 12, 14; stumbling blocks to, 13; survey of, 7-14
Strickland, Rennard, 54
Suicides, 21, 23

Superfund Amendments and Reauthorization Act (1986),
    64, 68
Supremacy Clause, 58, 59
Supreme Court (Kansas), gaming and, 41
Supreme Court (New Mexico), gaming and, 41
Supreme Court (U.S.), 75; IGRA and, 43, 44; mineral rights
    and, 34; state-tribal relations and, 2, 18, 19; taxation
    and, 48; waste disposal and, 66; water rights and, 55, 57
Swinomish, salmon fishery of, 36

T

Tano, Mervyn: environmental regulations and, 66
Taxation, 2, 8, 18, 36, 75; agreements on, 9, 45-52, 73;
    controversies about, 45; double, 48; resolving conflicts
    about, 48-49; revenues from, 45, 52; state-tribal relations
    and, v, 11, 13, 50-51; *See also* Various taxes by name
Taxation on Indian Reservations (Erickson and Martin), 45
Texas, Native American population of, 2; tax issues in, 47
Tigua, sales tax and, 47
Timber-fish-wildlife (TFW) agreement, 60-61
Timber/lumbering, 8, 36
Title 18 (U.S. Code), section 1151, on Indian Country, 4
Tobacco, taxes on, 47, 49, 50, 51, 52
Tourism, 12, 34, 36
Transportation Research Center (Indiana University), 69
Treaties, 5, 46; importance of, 4, 12
Treaty Indian Tribes of Western Washington, on TFW, 60
Tribal colleges, 27-28
Tribal economies, indicators of, 35
Tribal Education Code, 25
Tribal Foster Care Services (4-E) (Montana), 30
Tribal Government Assistance Program (Oklahoma), 33
Tribal governments, differences in, 3; state-tribal relations
    and, 19, 75; taxes by, 45, 48, 49
Tribal Nations of Montana, The, 75
Tribal/State Tobacco Tax Compact (1992) (Oklahoma), 51
Tribal Tax Status Act (1982), 46
Tribes, federal government and, 18; reservations and, 3-4;
    state legislatures and, 18
Tureen, Tom, 33

U

Uintah, mineral rights and, 34
Understanding, improving, 13, 14, 19
Unemployment, 4, 37
Unemployment compensation (FUTA), 46
U.S. vs. Washington (1971), 59
Use taxes, 47
Utah, health care in, 23-24; natural resources protection in,
    34; sovereignty issues in, 9; tax issues in, 48
Ute Mountain Ute, economic development and, 34

W

Warm Springs Confederated Tribes, tax compact with, 52

Washington, environmental regulations in, 65; fishing rights in, 36, 57-60; gaming in, 9, 40, 41, 43; hunting/fishing/wildlife accords in, 12, 58; intergovernmental agreements in, 12; Native American economy in, 4; sovereignty issues in, 9, 13; tax issues in, 50; timber industry in, 36

Washington vs. Confederated Salish and Kootenai, Clean Water Act, and, 65

Washington vs. Washington State Commercial Passenger Fishing Vessel Association (1979), 59

Waste disposal, 1, 2, 8, 18, 63, 66-67

Water rights, 8, 54; settling, 12, 55-57; tribal claims to, 16-17

Western Governors' Association, IGRA and, 42

White Earth Reservation Tribal Council, 24; direct-mail fund raising and, 34

White Mountain Apache, tourism and, 34

Wilkerson, Bill, 60

Wilkinson, Charles, 45; on state-tribal relations, 5; on treaties, 4

Williams vs. Lee, 2

Wilson, Pete: Peace bill and, 67

Winters case (1908), 55

Winters Doctrine, 55, 56

Wisconsin, economic development in, 33, 34; education in, 26; environmental regulations in, 65; foster care/child protection in, 11; gaming in, 40, 41, 42; health care in, 24; hunting/fishing/ wildlife accords in, 12, 17, 58; sovereignty issues in, 19; tax issues in, 11, 48, 50

Women, Infants and Children's Programs, IHB and, 23

Wyoming, foster care/child protection in, 11; tribal governments in, 3

Z

Zoning issues, 58, 66

ABOUT THE AUTHORS

James B. Reed is a program principal in the Energy, Science and Natural Resources Program at the National Conference of State Legislatures. He specializes in transportation, hazardous and radioactive materials and Native American environmental issues and has written more than 30 articles, reports and books. He staffed the NCSL Task Force on State-Tribal Relations from 1990 to 1993. Before coming to NCSL in 1988, Mr. Reed worked for the Texas Advisory Commission on Intergovernmental Relations, the Texas Legislature and former U.S. senator and treasury secretary Lloyd Bentsen. He earned a B.A. in political science from Colorado College in Colorado Springs and a master's degree in public administration from the LBJ School of Public Affairs at the University of Texas at Austin. His e-mail address is jim.reed@NCSL.org.

Judy A. Zelio is a senior policy specialist in NCSL's Fiscal Affairs Program, where she has worked since 1988. She specializes in state-local and state-tribal affairs as well as state tax and budget issues and has written a number of articles, reports and books on these topics. She staffed the NCSL Task Force on State-Tribal Relations from 1990 to 1993 and the State-Local-Tribal Relations Committee of the Assembly on State Issues in 1994. Currently she staffs the National Association of Legislative Fiscal Officers. She holds a bachelor's degree in history and political science from the University of Montana and a master's degree in anthropology from the University of Colorado. She can be reached by e-mail at judy.zelio@NCSL.org.